500 DAYS

Apache Australis
June 1984 – May 1987

500 DAYS

Around the World on a
Twelve Foot Yacht

by Serge Testa

Published by Trident Press
101 Pie Street
Aspley, Qld 4034, Australia

ISBN No: 0 7316 4849 8

First Published in Australia 1988

Contents

Maps

To my family,
for their help and understanding.

Chapter 1

SAILING OFF

Enjoying good winds, *Acrohc* sailed through the smooth blue waters of the Indian Ocean under a bright and welcoming sun. I was half way between Darwin and the Cocos Islands, a thousand miles from anywhere and after a month at sea, the feeling of being in the middle of nowhere still amazed me.

I was also enjoying the satisfaction one has when a plan finally comes together, to say nothing of the great feeling of sailing the open sea. Some playful dolphins visited me, staying an hour or so before swimming sway. They left me with a companion, a small, striped pilot fish. It was fun to see it darting through the waters chasing small prey but always returning to *Acrohc*.

Two days earlier, I had passed a cargo ship and used the VHF radio to send a message that would be relayed home. It read, 'Position 13°13' South, 116°17' West. All well on *Acrohc*. Love, Serge.' I knew those few words would make my family happy.

I had heard about the Cocos Islands, but so far they were just a minute spot on the chart; a place I had to find somewhere in the vast ocean. This was the first time that I had to rely on my sextant skills. The islands were the first place outside Australia that I was to visit with *Acrohc* and they would be followed by a lot more new places and a lot more water before my return to Brisbane.

That day, I estimated it would take about two weeks to reach land and the comforts I was missing at sea...if the fair winds held. The cyclone season had already started. It was January and not the best time to sail in these waters, but I knew *Acrohc* could withstand the worst weather so I wasn't too worried.

However less than two weeks later, on the 44th day of that passage, the winds gradually changed direction and blew harder and harder, lifting the waves until they were crashing over the bow; I could no longer keep the hatch open.

As the winds increased, I reduced sail until there was just enough to keep going forward. Soon the waves were higher than *Acrohc* herself and were coming down solidly, smashing over the cabin. The heat and humidity in the cabin became almost intolerable. The worst waves were not the ones that crashed over the boat but those that hit the hull at incredible speeds. I had to hang on tightly to prevent myself from being thrown about inside. *Acrohc* was leaning at 45 degrees and as these fast moving waves slammed against her, everything inside including me was jolted violently sideways—it was impossible to sleep or even rest.

I suspected that I was dealing with a cyclone. I knew *Acrohc* would survive, but I wondered how much more of this hell I could take without going mad. Why was I there, I asked myself. What made me take on such an adventure? Maybe I was mad. But I don't think I'm a masochist and I have never been suicidal, so why had I put myself in this situation?

All I wanted was to cruise around the world. But surely there were easier ways to do that. Why did I have to choose the hard way?

* * * * *

I had been thinking about it for some time. Then one day, in our small workshop, I finally decided to place the order for the materials I needed to build *Acrohc*. But it was only when the 200 kilos of marine grade aluminium were delivered on to the floor of the workshop that

I realized I was really going to build *Acrohc*. Until then, it had been nothing but an idea that was slowly forming in my mind. Now I had a pile of plates and bars on the floor. I didn't have any drawings—the plans were in my mind. It wasn't that I didn't believe in drawings, but I was the designer, builder and owner and I new exactly what I wanted.

So I started shaping and welding, cutting off and extending; modifying the design again and again. I changed the shape of the keel many times until I felt that it was right. Each feature, like the lines of the hull, the rudder, or the mast length, had to 'look' right. How could I have put that on paper beforehand?

Gradually the pile of metal on the floor became a boat. The rigging went on and then I began the fitting out. Before long, I ended up with a nice little boat that was to take me around the world. I felt proud and happy, already dreaming of tiny tropical islands, as I gave her a bright coat of yellow paint.

*****

On the 9th of June, 1984, I launched my mini yacht on the Brisbane River, where I was to start the long voyage. My older brother, Henry, remembers my excitement as I rowed the small, inflatable dinghy over to *Acrohc* when she was afloat for the first time. I couldn't help shouting, 'I'm free, I'm free', as the realization hit me that my new home wasn't attached to anything and I was free to wander.

Only close family and a few friends were present at the launching. Only they knew that I wanted to sail around the world and establish a new world record for a circumnavigation in the smallest boat. Apart from telling close relatives and friends, I kept quiet about my ambition and I especially didn't tell the media as I thought they'd be skeptical; even my own family wasn't convinced that I'd go through with it.

In fact, no-one could understand why I'd built a boat less than 12 feet long, with a 1.5 metre draft, six watertight compartments and as

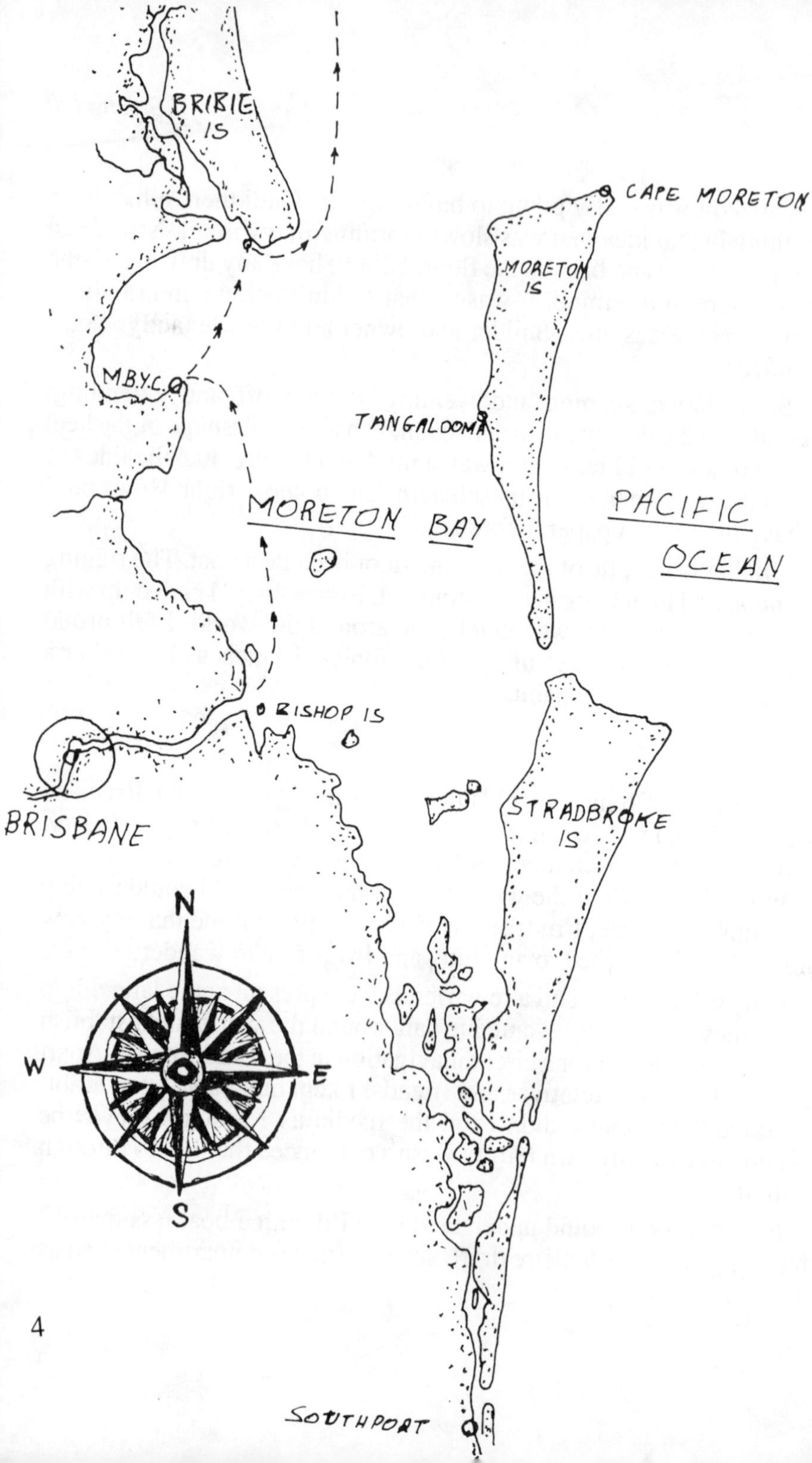

BRIBIE IS

CAPE MORETON

MORETON IS

M.B.Y.C.

TANGALOOMA

MORETON BAY

PACIFIC OCEAN

BISHOP IS

BRISBANE

STRADBROKE IS

N
W   E
S

4

SOUTHPORT

solid as a tank, for what they thought would be sailing around Moreton Bay. I heard people say many times that I must be crazy. And even at that stage I wasn't sure if it was feasible. I knew I had a strong and seaworthy boat but, after all, she was only 11 feet 10 inches long. How would she react to big waves, storms or even cyclones? Would she ever capsize? And would I be able to put up with the continuous pounding and rolling or would I end up as crazy as people thought I was? The best way to find out was to try!

Two days after the launching of *Acrohc* I decided to set out quietly, just in case I couldn't go through with it and so I wouldn't lose too much face if I failed . . . although the worst blow if I did fail would be to my self-esteem.

At first *Acrohc* sailed well on her maiden voyage down the Brisbane River. The favourable current and the small 4HP outboard motor helped us make good progress. But I experienced my first problem just halfway down the river when *Acrohc* suddenly veered out of control and almost hit a bridge pylon. Because she was so short with rather a tall mast for her size, she needed perfect sail balance. I discovered that the sail area was not set forward enough and that it only took a gust of wind to point her in the wrong direction and out of control. As I suspected, the modifications were not yet finished.

As a short term remedy to this problem, I reduced sail, but this also reduced speed. The only way to really improve things was to add a bowsprit which would take the genoa 60 centimetres forward. I got around to adding the bowsprit later in the trip.

I had no other problems on the river journey, the remainder of which *Acrohc* completed effortlessly.

We entered Moreton Bay which is sheltered from the open sea by islands; a perfect place to learn more about my new boat. There I discovered that her top speed was five knots in calm water (one knot is sailing at one sea mile per hour, or 1.8 kilometres per hour) and that she could point at 30 degrees to the wind but performed much better at 45 degrees, which meant that I could sail to windward fairly well.

I also discovered that the self-steering worked well, a pleasant surprise as I had designed it myself, somewhat differently from the norm. Normally in a self-steering mechanism, the vane moves a trim tab (a sort of small rudder), which in turn pushes the main rudder, but I believed that with *Acrohc's* low speed, direct action was better. The best thing about my self-steering system was that it could be set from inside the cabin. Via a system of cables, I could adjust the vane simply by turning the handle located behind the seat.

There was also an internal tiller coming through the deck which was connected by a complicated system of tubes and hinges and made steering possible while sitting on the bunk with the hatch closed—a nice feature for rainy days. For better weather I had another tiller on deck.

The two furling sails could also be controlled from inside. Their lines fed through six winches on deck with their handles inside the cabin. Two winches held the genoa lines and one rolled the foresail in or out of the furling system. This meant that I could reduce or let the headsail out according to wind strength. The mainsail rolled onto the boom via another winch, the halyard to hoist this sail went onto yet another and the sixth winch was to set the main. Six winches were all I needed to handle the sails at sea.

It hadn't been easy to make the deck watertight where the handles came through, but the nylon bushes that I'd fitted as seals gave good results. In fact, it was only towards the end of the trip that the bushes began to wear a little and let a few drops of water in.

All of these innovations were made to allow me to manoeuvre the boat while the hatch was closed, so that I'd keep as dry as possible in bad weather.

My destination that day, my first port of call, was Scarborough, a small harbour several kilometres north of Brisbane but still in Moreton Bay. However, it was dark and raining when I arrived and I had forgotten about a line of rocks that extended out from the shore! Luckily only the keel hit the rocks and *Acrohc* got off lightly, but even so I still couldn't find the set of green and red lights marking the entrance to the small harbour. Finally I saw a red light and, sailing towards it, ran aground. This time we were stuck fast. Two minutes later when the red light passed me I realized that it was not the harbour light at all but a fishing boats's navigation light. It was a good start! By this time it was really dark, I was aground, and I had no idea where I was. There was nothing for it but to throw out the anchor, wait for the tide and get some sleep; morning would shed light on the problem. This was my first lesson—never arrive anywhere after dark!

The next morning I was surprised to see the breaker wall of the harbour and the harbour entrance just two hundred metres to my right.

Some time later, anchored in the harbour and after a cup of coffee, I took out my log book and entered, 'Scarborough, first stop' and some details of the trip. From that day on I entered each day's events in the log.

My family came to see me for the last time before I was to sail north along the Queensland coast. I could see that my parents weren't in the mood to celebrate my departure and only then I realized why they hadn't shown much concern about my undertaking the trip. Even at the launching of *Acrohc* they hadn't really believed that I was going to sail any further than Moreton Bay. But now that I was out of Brisbane waters and saying that all was going well, it struck them that I was really going to go on and they lost hope of my giving up my 'suicidal idea'.

It was late and the yacht club was closed so we sat outside on the quay and had a farewell drink. I knew I was going to see them again before I left Australia but it was still a moving moment.

My younger brother, John, reminded me for the hundredth time to tie myself to the boat whenever the hatch was open. His main concern was that I would fall overboard and be left behind with nothing but what I was wearing . . . if, indeed, I was wearing anything!

Henry carefully examined the boat from bow to stern, yet again, looking for flaws. He was almost (but not quite) satisfied when he didn't find anything. I promised everyone again that I would be careful, that they shouldn't worry and that I'd keep in touch.

Early the next morning I set off for Bribie Island which is just outside Moreton Bay. It was winter and the beaches, usually crowded with weekenders, looked deserted and sad.

I arrived at the Island just before dark without mishap. *Acrohc* was slowly proving what she was capable of.

The next day I headed for Mooloolaba harbour. After making an average speed of four knots, thanks to good winds, I tied up for the night at the yacht club's jetty. Then I contacted a friend, Lee, whom I'd got to know when building a 45 foot boat for him. He invited me for dinner and a shower, insisting, 'You'll never know when you can take another shower!' And how right he was.

Throughout my trip I often recalled his words and many times I would have paid a fortune for the luxury of standing under a fresh-water shower.

I left early the next morning for Noosa where late that afternoon I anchored in a nice sandy cove. I should have stayed at anchor there but I decided instead to enter the river, which would take me to the town itself so that I could have a walk ashore. (Throughout the voyage, even after a short trip, I always liked to go for a walk and

enjoy a celebratory drink—of course, I often made new friends and one drink became many!).

To get to the town of Noosa, however, I had to sail over a sandbar at the mouth of the river. *Acrohc* grazed the bar but luckily the waves pushed us over stopping us from getting stuck. Once in the river, I missed the channel and, again, ran aground. So there we stayed waiting for the morning high tide to free us.

It was still light, so to salvage some pride I threw out a fishing line so that it would appear to the crews of nearby fishing boats that I was there for a spot of fishing.

On the morning's tide we got off the damned sandbank. A passing fisherman told me where the channel to leave the river was, as by that stage I'd completely lost interest in going for a walk and having a drink. In fact, I wasn't even tempted by the lure of Noosa's main tourist attraction, its nudist beach.

I ran aground again, trying to recross the bar, and this time I couldn't pretend to be fishing. A motor boat came along side and one of the men aboard called, 'Anything wrong, mate?'.

Feeling somewhat disgusted with myself I asked if they could give me a tow to '...just get me out of here!'

Thankfully, they spared me any humour at my expense, however, as we were in only half a metre of water and *Acrohc* needed one and a half to float, they had to drag us over the bar. From this indignity I learned another valuable lesson—never go anywhere doubtful. Funnily enough, though, it was a lesson I often forgot!

Mishaps behind me, I headed for Wide Bay, another day's run up the coast. I anchored that evening off an isolated beach. It was a big, open bay and very windy, definitely not the best place to spend a night. But, with yesterday's events fresh in my mind, there was no way that I would even consider crossing the bar before daylight. I'd just have to wait for morning to continue on down the channel between the mainland and Fraser Island (famous for its sandy beaches and for being a nature reserve).

I had hoped to meet up with the yacht *Moonshine* as her crew had promised to lead *Acrohc* through the channel, but when morning dawned with no sight of *Moonshine*, I decided to attempt it by myself.

I approached the bar extremely cautiously. If I missed the channel I'd be in serious trouble; the big waves would easily roll me onto the beach. There was little wind so, with the motor going flat out, we almost surfed into the channel. But as I turned to follow the channel a wave hit *Acrohc* and my little motor stalled.

For a split second I panicked—I had to restart the motor before the waves threw us to the edge of the channel. Luckily a few wild pulls on the starting cord got it running again and I relaxed as we motored peacefully through the waters of Sandy Straights. I hoped that I wouldn't have to rely on the motor too often.

It was a different world in the channel. No wind and no waves. It was just like a lagoon. In fact, from here until the northernmost tip of Australia, I would be sailing through mainly sheltered waters, protected by either islands or the Great Barrier Reef.

Soon after getting over the bar, *Moonshine* arrived. Her skipper shouted over to me that they hadn't expected me to arrive at the bar that morning, that, in fact, they hadn't expected *Acrohc* to sail so fast. This was to be the first of many underestimations of *Acrohc's* speed. After a chat over the water with *Moonshine's* crew, I continued on.

I reached Tin Can Bay that evening and had to spend the night there as, despite the clear waters of the bay, I managed to run aground again. And the same thing happened the next evening when I reached the mangrove covered coastline of Vernon Point. However, it is easy to run aground in the Sandy Straights; the name says it all. It's a vast area of shallow water, dotted with sandbanks. The channels between the banks are marked with beacons but these beacons are placed so far apart that whenever I passed a beacon it often took half a mile's sailing to sight the next one. Being on a boat that lay so low in the water didn't help matters either.

I didn't feel too ashamed of running aground so often. Very few yachts get through the Straights without grounding; even the local trawlers get stuck occasionally.

Once, when *Acrohc* was lying peacefully aground, heeling only slightly, I decided to make the most of the early evening by relaxing on the open hatch with a cup of coffee. There wasn't a ripple on the water and not a sound to be heard (except for the occasional mosquito); we were miles away from anything.

Suddenly, I heard a loud breathing coming from behind *Acrohc*. It gave me a hell of a fright. But it was no sea monster, just a friendly turtle coming up for air. During the trip, I often heard odd sounds. Sometimes it was turtles, sometimes dolphins, but I never got such a fright again.

I spent one more night aground as a result of trying (after dark!) to find the channel into the river that leads to the small country town of Burrum Heads.

The following morning, upriver, I met Vince, a cruising friend from Brisbane who had been waiting for me to catch up with him. He had a 28 foot yacht and was also on his way north. He was going at a much slower pace though and had no intention of sailing around the world.

The two days that I spent anchored in the river at Burrum Heads gave me a good chance to relax and take a few long walks along nearby beaches before Vince and I left for Bundaberg, the 'City of Rum'.

We left the calm waters of Sandy Straights behind and in the ensuing unsheltered stretch of the coast, the sea became much rougher. I could still sail along fairly well though and I was still able to make coffee on the spirit stove. However, locked inside the cabin, I didn't realize just how rough the sea had become until I heard a whistle. I opened the hatch and saw Vince's boat about ten metres away. He shouted, 'I'm not going to put up with this. I'm going back!'

I understood his decision. It's not very pleasant in an open cockpit in bad weather as I well know from experience with my first boat, an old 25 foot wooden sloop bought 10 years earlier in Sydney.

When I had first seen her she wasn't a pretty sight, despite being out of the water and thus showing her beautiful lines. There was no dry rot on the hull and without hesitation I paid the asking price of one thousand dollars. The low price was because she had sunk at her moorings and been left underwater for a few months, weighed down by a half a ton of mud. In fact, she had become home to a million or so barnacles, a two metre moray eel and dozens of small fish.

It wasn't until I started work on her that I realized a lot of her ribs needed replacing. The cabin was also falling apart and I actually ended up having to rebuild the entire topside. But six months of hard work rewarded me with a home on the water, proudly renamed *Lisa* after my only niece.

The idea was that I would be able to travel the world without carrying luggage or having to look for accommodation wherever I arrived. My knowledge of boats, seamanship or sailing was nil. I knew I liked the sea but my only experience of oceans had been looking at the water from the deck of large liners! The word 'cruising' was unfamiliar to me but I was to learn that it was a world of its own.

In fact, a 'yachtie' is a sort of 'Gypsy of the oceans' but, contrary to what many think, it's not always an easy life. However, I soon got to like the idea and before long, by trial and error, I had learned how to set sails and what all the bits and pieces were on my boat and how to use them. I bought a book on coastal navigation from which I learned enough of the basic skills to set out on my own.

When *Lisa* was ready to sail, my brother John agreed to help me sail her from Sydney to Brisbane. On our second day out we got caught in a bad storm and on that day I swore I'd never set foot on a boat again. I did, of course, and I've sworn the same thing again.

Meanwhile, back on *Acrohc* being closed inside the cabin made rough weather easier to cope with, especially with the internal winches. The seas during the trip to Bundaberg were very choppy, with winds up to 35 knots but at least they were blowing in the right direction. It was also very cold and I learned later that for the first time in a hundred years it had snowed in Queensland.

I was relieved to arrive and anchor in the tree sheltered river that leads to Bundaberg. It was much warmer there than on the open sea and in the warmth of the cabin I made myself a hot meal of vegetable soup. I fell asleep happy knowing that *Acrohc* could take some rough weather, though I was aware that we could be facing a lot worse when sailing in the truly open sea.

In the middle of the night I was awakened by a woman shouting, 'Hello yellow boat with stripes!' *Acrohc* didn't have any stripes, but the shouts sounded serious enough for me to jump out of bed and leave the warmth of the cabin. When I opened the hatch I saw a rusty trawler on one side of *Acrohc* and a big white yacht on the other; they were both drifting toward us and it looked like *Acrohc* was going to be sandwiched. I wasn't fully awake, but I didn't have to be to realize that I had to pick up the anchor and move quickly without argument. (Later I was told that the boats' anchors had become tangled.)

I met the white yacht *Freebooter* again the next morning when I was trying to motor upriver to the city. My outboard couldn't cope with the strong winds so, helpfully, they gave me a tow for a few miles and I forgave them my rude awakening the previous night!

In Bundaberg, I found the materials to make the much needed bowsprit. The new bowsprit not only improved the sailing but was also a good place to store my new CQR anchor. I bought this plough-like anchor, which is suitable for most seabeds, to use as the main anchor. (The traditional 'fisherman's anchor' worked best in weed covered seabeds.)

I also modified the headsail furling system. Originally, the sail rolled around a wire rope but this was not efficient as, when only half the sail was let out, its shape was too distorted. I put an alloy track around the cable for the sail to roll onto; this way no matter how much sail was left out, it was still efficient and had the proper shape of a sail.

One day whilst still anchored in Bundaberg, *Freebooter's* crew came on board to have a look at *Acrohc*. The crew from the *Ben Kelly*, a yacht I knew from Brisbane, also joined us. Nine people altogether came on board resulting in a party, on deck of course. Later in the voyage that record of nine was to be broken.

I discovered that one of the nice things about having such a small boat was that I could tie up to the dock with the dinghies; *Acrohc* was, after all, the same size as a dinghy! The other yachts had to tie on to a mooring in the middle of the river and pay a fee.

I spent a week in Bundaberg before leaving on my first overnight trip to a place called 1770, named after the year Captain Cook landed there. There was nothing much of interest at 1770 except for a caravan park and kiosk but I did meet up with Vince again. I wasn't very keen on the place but I stayed a week as I'd promised to wait for *Ben Kelly* to catch up. I spent most of the time there chatting to other yachties.

When they finally arrived and after another party, I left my friends behind, motoring out of the wide and shallow river.

I ran aground again—this was getting ridiculous! However, this time I got off easily by throwing an anchor out as far as I could and pulling myself off. Of course, *Acrohc's* weight of only 500 kilos helped and I used this method successfully a number of times to get off sandbanks.

On my way to Cape Capricorn unfavourable winds made me stop overnight at Pancake Creek. At this stage of my journey I still had

Dolphins at play along the Coral Coast

the option of making such stops, but later on I would have to battle out any weather or tricky situations.

The next morning I thought about going ashore to pick some of the wild lemons that I'd been told grew there, or perhaps to collect some oysters from the rocks, but I decided to sail on. Overnight the wind had changed so I left Pancake Creek with a strong following wind which held all the way to Cape Capricorn. With the good wind I averaged four and half knots with a top speed of seven knots although that was 'surfing' down a wave. I was getting near the tropics and warmer weather.

Next stop was Great Keppel Island, a well known and beautiful tourist spot. It has fine sandy beaches and is covered with tropical vegetation. I would have enjoyed spending a couple of days ashore among the coconut trees, but on the second day a storm blew up and I was stuck aboard *Acrohc* because the wind was blowing straight towards the rocks and I was anchored just outside them. To lift anchor and attempt to move was too dangerous so I was forced to stay there until the wind changed, with *Acrohc* dancing a jig on every wave. There wasn't any danger and there wasn't much I could do but trust the anchor to hold and be patient. A few times I was tempted to make a move out of there, if only to be more comfortable, but I kept reminding myself that it was going to be a long trip and that I shouldn't take any unnecessary risks. Patience is an important part of sailing.

I was able to make a move the next morning so I resumed my trip up the coast making overnight stops. I stopped at five more islands before reaching the harbour at Mackay. I tied up for the night at the jetty where, for the first time, I experienced the five metre tide found on that part of the coast. As the tide ran out, the jetty became higher and higher above me and I had to lengthen the lines gradually throughout the night. By morning the jetty was higher than the top of the mast!

Sailing on, I reached Shute Harbour but I decided not to stop there after looking at the dozens of charter yachts that filled the harbour. *Acrohc*, a cruising yacht, would definitely look out of place there so I pressed on to Airlie Beach where I immediately felt at home. Hundreds of cruising yachts from all over the world were anchored there and I was reunited with many friends. Every day another yacht arrived. Sometimes it was an old acquaintance and sometimes a yacht I'd met on the way up from Brisbane.

We talked of distant ports and ocean passages which made me all the more eager to get on with my trip. Just the thought of anchoring *Acrohc* in a foreign port excited me more and more.

But the other reason I stayed so long at Airlie Beach was because it is such a pretty place. Right in the heart of the Whitsundays, it is surrounded by resorts that give the entire area a holiday feeling. Apart from visiting two of the resorts, I sailed to the nearby Nara Inlet to spend three days on deserted Hook Island. Here I discovered lots of rock oysters and beautiful bush walks. One bush walk led me to a cave that was home to Aborigines and their paintings long ago. The cave paintings and the well sheltered natural harbour combine to make Nara Inlet a very popular yachties' attraction. In fact, Nara Inlet is a preferred anchorage when cyclones threaten the Whitsundays.

The beautiful, unspoiled island covered by dense vegetation and with interesting reefs that can be seen through the clear warm water make the whole area a cruising paradise. I spent a relaxing month there cruising around the islands, preparing *Acrohc* and myself for the following leg of the journey.

The preparations included giving *Acrohc* a new coat of antifouling paint and, at last, painting on her name. This was required for her registration which I would also need to do before I left Australia. The boat's name, *Acrohc Australis* and her port of registration, Brisbane, had to be painted in letters 10 centimetres high on the transom to comply with regulations and I confess to having a slight problem fitting it all on the back of the boat.

The name came to be when I was building her. I liked the name *Australis* but there were already many boats with that name. While trying to find another name, I asked my mother what she would call the boat. She answered me in the Italian dialect we often speak at home, 'What boat? Oh, you mean that thing!' The translation of 'thing' is '*Acrohc*', so my boat became *Acrohc Australis*, a strange name perhaps but then it was for a strange boat.

While I was still in the Whitsundays, I couldn't resist entering my unique boat in the famous Whitsunday Fun Race.

About 500 boats took part and it didn't matter who won as long as everyone had fun. When I entered the race, the official made no comment about *Acrohc's* size but there were plenty during the race!

One of the rules is that the boat must have a figurehead, preferably a real naked or near naked girl. Although I would have liked one on my boat, *Acrohc* was too small and was sadly exempted from this rule. I won a prize though—not for being first or last but for being the smallest boat in the race. The big bottle of rum I received was not only used to celebrate my last farewell to friends who were returning south for the summer to escape the cyclone season, but it was also used to celebrate my intention of sailing around the world which I announced there.

The media lost no time labelling *Acrohc* 'a sailing bathtub', but my yachting friends all thought it was feasible, though none of them envied me.

I still had to test myself to see if I could cope with the long and lonely legs of the trip, but at least by this time I knew *Acrohc* was up to it. However, having told everyone of my intentions, I had no choice any more.

PACIFIC OCEAN

CORAL SEA

GREAT BARRIER REEF

BRISBANE
MOOLOOLABA
NOOSA
WIDE BAY
GREAT SANDY STRAITS
BURRUM HDS
BUNDABERG
GLADSTONE
ROCKHAMPTON

TROPIC OF CAPRICORN

MACKAY
WHITSUNDAY
TOWNSVILLE
CAIRNS
COOKTOWN
C. YORK
THURSDAY IS.
N. GUINEA

ARAFURA SEA

GULF OF CARPENTARIA

QUEENSLAND

NORTHERN TERRITORY

DARWIN
V. DIEMEN'S GULF

WESTERN AUS.

Chapter 2

BARRIER REEF TO ARAFURA SEA

The 15th of September, the day after the big race, I left Airlie Beach. It had been more than three months since *Acrohc's* maiden voyage down the Brisbane River and I decided that the easy going days were over. This day hopping up the Queensland coast must stop or the circumnavigation would take 10 years.

So, the night of the 15th was spent under sail. Until then I'd only slept on *Acrohc* while at anchor, but I must say that I had no trouble at all sleeping that night.

However, on the second day I had to make an unplanned and unwilling stop at Cape Bowling Green (probably named for its blanket of lush, green grass). My plan had been to sleep at night and wake every hour for quick checks on wind changes. But early that morning I slept through and was awoken by a thud from the hull. Whilst I had been sleeping the wind had changed, steering us towards the beach where the one metre swell had pushed *Acrohc* onto hard sand. To make matters worse, the tide was running out. Unlike my previous brushes with sandbanks and running aground, I didn't have the option of sleeping it out or waiting for the tide to rise; this time I had to act fast.

Grabbing an anchor, I dived into the swell and swam as far out to sea as the line would take me. Then, after dropping the anchor, I swam back to *Acrohc* and climbed halfway up the mast. Using my weight as a counter-balance, I hauled on the line. This made *Acrohc* lean over and free her keel from the sand. Then, hauling her a few metres out to sea and using the first anchor to hold her, I swam out again to put the other anchor further out. I repeated this exercise six times and throughout the swimming and hauling I loudly cursed myself. 'You stupid fool. Never let this happen again,' are the only words printable.

Luckily *Acrohc* was sturdy enough to cope with such a battering and she came through the ordeal without any damage although inside was a mess with everything wet through. I, on the other hand, had sore and blistered hands from pulling on the lines. My whole body ached from effort and fatigue.

I can't ever remember, either before or since, being so angry and upset with myself and I vowed never to let something like that happen again...another promise, I'm sorry to say, I failed to keep.

I was looking forward to sailing in an open sea where at least the risk of running aground was minimal.

The following night I arrived in Townsville, the unofficial capital of Northern Queensland. Michael, a friend I had made whilst cruising the Whitsundays, had offered me the use of his mooring free of charge and I took him up on his kind offer.

I stayed in Townsville for ten days, catching up with friends, mail and the media, and arranging for *Acrohc's* registration to be processed by a port official. (This was so that I could get the necessary registration papers to legally leave Australian waters—I only got the papers a few weeks before I left Australia.)

After a farewell party held at Townsville's boat club, which was organized and filmed by the Australian A.B.C. Television Network, I set off for Cairns, the closest city to the Barrier Reef. Cairns is well known by big game fishermen, but it was important to me as it was the last big city for supplies that I'd visit before Darwin (from where I would leave Australia).

It took two days of easy sailing to reach Cairns. I was starting to know my boat well and was settling into a daily routine. Although my cooking facilities were limited, preparing meals was not a problem. As each leg so far had been quite short, fresh supplies such as meat and vegetables had kept well enough in the lockers. Later I would learn how to store foodstuffs efficiently during the longer stretches at sea.

I slept at anchor most nights but I found sleeping in *Acrohc* at sea quite comfortable; by this time, I'd become used to living in her small cabin. In good weather I could sail with the hatch open, sitting on the hatch itself which converted into a seat. In rougher weather I stayed inside, sitting or lying on the bunk. There was enough room to move around comfortably, but certainly not enough to stand. Space was a precious commodity, all of it being used as efficiently as possible.

As I sat on the bunk, the spirit stove was on my left and next to the stove were the fresh and saltwater pumps. On my right were basic navigation instruments, including an electronic log which told me the correct speed. By checking this I knew when to trim the sails to get the best possible speed from *Acrohc*. On the same panel were switches for both the navigation and cabin lights and a voltmetre which kept me informed of the condition of the battery (a 12 volt heavy duty car battery).

I kept the hand bearing compass on the right. The main compass was fitted above the chart table, away from any possible magnetic interference from electrical equipment such as the echo-sounder. The sounder was theoretically my most important piece of equipment. It was supposed to stop me from running aground but as I had learned from bitter experience, it didn't work properly and try as I might, I could never set it properly. (Later on in the trip I replaced it but I got doubtful readings from the replacement sounder too. Whether *Acrohc's* metallic hull had anything to do with it I still don't know.)

A central, lidded chart table doubled as my dining table. It could be slid out of the way between the bunk and the clothes locker when not in use. It also stored the navigation charts away from water splashes and drips.

The main food lockers were behind the seat. Other lockers were situated along the side of the bunk. In these I kept medical equipment, tools and all necessary bits and pieces. One of these lockers housed distress flares and a strobe torchlight. The strobe light was for use in busy shipping lanes. I also kept a radio direction finder (RDF), binoculars, a camera, a sail repair kit and a distress beacon in this locker, carrying the latter only (I hoped) for peace of mind. When activated, the distress beacon's signals would be picked up by aeroplanes passing within a range of a couple of hundred miles, the idea being for the pilots to alert the authorities to start a search. It was not a toy and it was only to be turned on in the event of an emergency, for example, if we were sinking.

The battery was in a locker in front of my feet, towards the front of the boat. Ropes, jerrycans and shoes were kept in the bow locker which was only accessible from the outside of the boat. The fresh water tank was below the bunk to keep the weight down. I had got used to using seawater for washing myself and I no longer minded using a bucket for a toilet. Mind you, in crowded anchorages it was best to use the bucket only at night. In good weather at sea I could simply lean over the side of the boat!

*****

I was well received at the Cairns Yacht Club where I stayed for two days. The two days were spent re-provisioning *Acrohc* and I left for Port Douglas fully stocked.

I celebrated my 34th birthday alone at sea, in the middle of nowhere. However, I celebrated again the following day at Port Douglas with some of the local fishermen who put me right as to the correct date! I was a day ahead of myself . . . I'd been going fast, but not faster than time itself.

The next day, anchored off Low Isles, a tourist spot, I caught myself a late but edible birthday present—two small fish. I was very pleased with myself; these were the first fish I'd managed to catch so far on the trip. I knew that I couldn't rely on my angling talents to keep me supplied with fish for dinner while at sea, this being my only 'fishy' triumph to date.

En route to Cooktown *Acrohc* had 30 to 40 knot following winds and a choppy sea.

As I arrived a yachtsman rowed out to meet me and yelled, as he threw me an unexpected but very welcome gift, 'Here! Anyone who can sail in this wind deserves a beer.' I agreed!

I anchored for two days in the river. The town had seen better days during the gold rush of the last century and when the First World War started it was still considered important enough to supply with arms to fend off a possible invasion. It was sent one cannon, three cannon balls and two rifles to counter any invading hordes. But luckily the enemy did not invade and was spared a violent encounter with this impressive arsenal. The 'arsenal' is now in the town's square, a monument to the invasion that never was.

From Cooktown, I day-sailed along the Barrier Reef, anchoring at small islands each evening. I couldn't sail at night in these waters, even using the sleep and hourly check method, as the danger of hitting a reef or meeting a cargo ship was very real. Even sailing during the day I had to stay alert at all times to avoid not only cargo ships but smaller obstacles like the turtles that would insist in swimming slowly across *Acrohc's* path . . . I didn't want to hurt such peaceful animals.

In the nearly abandoned gold mining town of Portland Roads, my anchor got stuck in the remains of an old jetty. Another yachtsman helped me haul up the huge piece of timber on which the anchor had caught fast. Thus the start for Haggerstone Island was delayed for a couple of hours and I arrived there at night so I couldn't see where I dropped the anchor. But instead of things going wrong I had a wonderful surprise in the morning.

25

I was anchored on the sheltered side of the island and beneath *Acrohc's* keel was the most beautiful display of coral I had ever seen. I could see every detail of the seabed which was entirely covered by a multitude of different types of vividly coloured coral dotted with starfish and giant clams. Many species of fish, as highly coloured as the reef, swam over and around the coral. I lifted anchor and for an hour drifted slowly, being careful not to disturb the water so that I could get a clear view of one of the world's wonders.

In total, the Reef stretches for almost 1,000 kilometres, sort of a giant and timeless jewel. Captain Cook must have marvelled when he discovered it 200 years ago, though his enjoyment may have been slightly tempered by having to navigate through the labyrinth of then uncharted channels. He nearly lost the *Endeavour* several times in the wonderful yet dangerous reef.

*****

Too soon I left the beautiful reef and its sheltered waters but I promised myself that one day I would visit the spot again.

Continuing north I caught a bird on the trawling line and, soon after, a sea snake—enough to make even the keenest fisherman give up.

On the way to Thursday Island, the northernmost part of Australia, I experienced strong winds, rough seas and rain. I arrived at Thursday Island sad to leave the Barrier Reef behind me but glad that there'd be no more day trips because of the danger from ships and reefs. From there on I could make longer passages and sail through the nights.

At most of my stopovers on the four month cruise up the Queensland coast, I was able to have only a brief look at the beautiful places I'd anchored at. Often I opted for staying on board simply for fear of wanting to stay longer. I had also visited only some of the many deserted islands and on those I did visit, my stays were all too brief. I would have loved to have been able to explore their surrounding reefs and marine life, or chat with the odd lighthouse keeper on the scattered islands.

There were many places I didn't stop at which were only accessible by boat. I could have explored inland rivers inhabited by saltwater crocodiles and visited pearl farms and remote settlements, but I came to the conclusion that it would take a lifetime to fully explore the Barrier Reef; *Acrohc* and I had to move on.

*****

Thursday Island is one of the better known islands in the Torres Straight. There some of the islanders still make their living from fishing or from catching sea turtles, but a lot of their old way of living seems to have disappeared. There were still a few pearl luggers anchored outside the island's open harbour, but these beautiful old sailing boats are no longer used for pearling.

There didn't seem to be any racial problems and everyone was friendly, but I found the island of little interest to me. After only three days there I was ready to set off on the next leg to Darwin, 800 miles across the Arafura Sea. This leg would prove whether I would be able to withstand loneliness without going mad.

As Thursday Island receded I made the first entry of this leg in the log:

October 23: Good progress, lots of waves due to the vast shallow sea, a little uncomfortable, but expect it to be easy trip of about 11 days.

October 24: Better, more reasonable winds, always coming from behind, usual first day sea sickness gone, starting to enjoy trip. I was never seriously seasick, but I was always a little sick for a day or so after a couple of days ashore.

October 25-26: Averaging eighty miles a day, getting used to not smoking. I had dumped my tobacco and pipe overboard just before I started the leg to try to give up smoking!

October 27: Sighted another ship today, have seen one almost everyday, they remind me that I'm not totally alone in the world.

Some yachts carry long range two way radios but I decided against having one as they use a lot of battery power.

October 28: Winds variable, made 20 miles at the most. I was navigating by 'dead reckoning' which means that I was working out how many miles were being travelled in a set direction. I was also using the radio direction finder which works by defining the direction of certain radio beacons that are usually situated on land. Basically it's just like a normal transistor radio, but instead of picking up radio broadcasting stations, it picks up signals being sent from set beacons. (Actually, an ordinary radio can be used and, in fact, I often used one.) By knowing the position of the beacons on the charts and by taking two or more readings, the position of the boat can be determined. Unfortunately it's not very accurate and in some areas the beacons are placed a bit too far apart.

October 29: Same winds, no sign of ships so I can sleep easier, not worried so much about being run over.

For the next three days I sailed into headwinds and was also becalmed several times.

AUSTRALIAN
PELICAN

October 30: Started drinking salt water, almost a litre. A French doctor, Dr. Alain Bombard, had written an article saying that this was possible. As part of his experiments, he had drifted across the Atlantic Ocean on a liferaft relying, to survive, on a certain percentage of saltwater. I wanted to experiment also in case the need arose, always rinsing my mouth out with a little fresh water afterwards so I wouldn't feel thirsty.

November 2: No wind at all. This was the eleventh day out of Thursday Island. Instead of arriving in Darwin as I'd hoped, I was just over halfway—in the middle of nowhere and hardly moving at all. This proved that I could not predict arrival times.

November 3: Getting used to drinking salt water, today drank one litre. It was also still very calm.

November 4: Some headwinds, made a bit of progress, Navy plane flew over us, but no-one heard my shouts for a cigarette. More than a litre today.

November 5: Getting upset about this stupid wind.

November 6: With the help of outboard entered shallows of Diemen Gulf, water suddenly became a clear green colour instead of the usual blue. Too close to land. Stopped drinking seawater. Now I knew drinking seawater was possible and I felt no side effects; But, then, it was only for one week.

November 7: 20 miles closer to Darwin, not going fast, but at least going forward.

On November 8, the seventeenth day after leaving Thursday Island, I was finally near Darwin. I was unable to go any further due to a strong tidal current so I anchored near an islet for the night and next morning motored the rest of the way up river to a marina just past the city. I happily anchored *Acrohc* amongst the other boats and went ashore. I asked where I could get cigarettes and a cold beer and after a short walk found myself in the city.

A couple of hours later I got back to *Acrohc* only to find her high and dry on a desert of mud; the tide strikes again! But *Acrohc* was used to being aground by then and anyway nothing could have upset me that day; I was on top of the world. I had spent 18 days alone at sea and I felt that I could have managed for a lot longer. I'd got used to having only myself for company after only a couple of days out of Thursday Island. Now I knew what it was like to be alone (although I wouldn't have minded having someone to talk to, especially a 'she'). This had been my major concern since starting the trip. I could modify the boat if and whenever necessary, but if I couldn't take being alone there would have been nothing else for it but to give up. It was quite a relief to find that I was up to the task.

While in Darwin, my major objective was to get *Acrohc* out of the water for a few weeks for antifouling and to do some work on her before the next big leg to the Cocos Islands. The marina had no space available for dry storage of boats and even when I assured the man in charge that *Acrohc* was only small, he remained unimpressed, 'That's what they all say.'

I eventually managed to convince him that *Acrohc* really only was 12 feet long so he found a spot for me. We winched *Acrohc* out of the water using a crane and secured her ashore.

It was close to Christmas and therefore the cyclone season. I wasn't keen on being in Darwin at that time of the year. Only ten years previously Darwin had been totally destroyed by Cyclone Tracey. So as far as I was concerned the sooner we were back at sea the better.

Actually, many believe that a boat is safer in the open sea during a cyclone. Others say that to be near land is safer, for the crew can always find safety ashore if a situation becomes too dangerous. But this means that very often the boat can be lost. I believe that at sea, and providing the boat is strong, it's simply a matter of putting up with the bad weather. Perhaps it all depends on just how much an individual trusts the boat, or perhaps it's simply a matter of whether one can afford the loss—for many, like me, the boat is all they own.

I lost no time in starting work on *Acrohc*. I strengthened anything that might break in bad weather; reinforcing the rigging with a few more cables, just in case I encountered a cyclone, and also installing an extra dorado vent for more ventilation in case I had to stay in the cabin for long periods.

After a week of work I returned to Brisbane, mostly to see my family for the last time before leaving Australia, but also to try to find sponsorship for the trip. Somewhat optimistically I started off by hitchhiking to save money. However, it was the rainy season and only a few vehicles were attempting the trip. The route was a mixture of deserts and floods and, running the gauntlet of lifts with people who were either dog tired from driving or just plain drunk, I often wondered if I'd reach Brisbane alive. Three days of waiting for this type of lift in hot, deserted locations was enough; I completed the trip by bus. I returned to Darwin by bus too . . . and without a sponsor!

*****

I felt guilty when I saw *Acrohc* again. Out of the water she seemed miserable as though she were trying to tell me that she wanted to be off again. The two weeks I'd spent away made me realize how fond of her I'd become.

I spent one more week preparing for the next leg. One of the most important tasks was shopping for provisions, working out how much I could store, how they would keep and how long they would last.

I decided to sail to the Cape of Good Hope via the Cocos Islands rather than through the Red Sea, which was notorious for its bad currents and winds; it was also a hotbed of political unrest. I read up on the winds and currents of the Indian Ocean and opted for going via South Africa.

So, my next stop would be 2,000 miles away, assuming, that is, that I could find the Cocos Islands in such a big ocean. I had just bought a couple of books on celestial navigation and a new sextant but although I knew how to work it, I had never used one at sea. There was also the risk of bad weather. For example, if I lost the mast in a cyclone, I would just have to drift with the current all the way to Africa.

I felt confident that *Acrohc* would never sink. The three millimetre alloy hull was strong enough to survive 'an encounter of the third kind' with quite a large ship. Being so small *Acrohc* would offer little resistance and would quite likely be pushed aside rather than crushed. And even if she was holed, the six watertight compartments would keep her afloat.

I calculated that to cope with any bad luck, I would need supplies for at least a year. I took a lot of tinned food and basic foodstuffs like rice, noodles, cheese, flour and milk powder. This, together with sprouts that I would grow to supply me with fresh vegetables, should provide enough food to eat decently for four to six months. If there was still no sign of land I could then live on rice, milk and sprouts for another six months.

I carried a hundred litres of fresh water in the water tank and another hundred litres in plastic containers which were stored in the bow locker. If I used no more than two litres a day this supply would last me for three months. Surely in three months there would be some rain to top up my supply and, if worse came to worst, I could always ask a passing ship for assistance or drink a bit of saltwater.

I was also well stocked up with medical supplies, following the advice from both my doctor and a chemist. I was ready for anything ranging from a headache to appendicitis. Seriously, I carried the local anaesthetic and scalpels necessary to operate on myself. I still don't know if I'd have had the guts to do it. I also carried a myriad of drugs ranging from painkillers to antibiotics, diarrhoea pills to malaria tablets and a goodly supply of multi-vitamins to supplement my diet.

While in Darwin I was adopted by a couple, Daniel and Anne-Marie, and their twins. I became one of the family and spent many pleasant evenings with them and on Christmas Day they gave a memorable party.

Daniel and Anne-Marie were willing helpers in my preparation of *Acrohc*. However, they often tried to convince me to stay on in Darwin until the end of the cyclone season, some four months later.

But I insisted that *Acrohc* was strong enough to withstand the roughest weather; I'd designed her that way, and, anyway, the chances of meeting a really bad cyclone were slim.

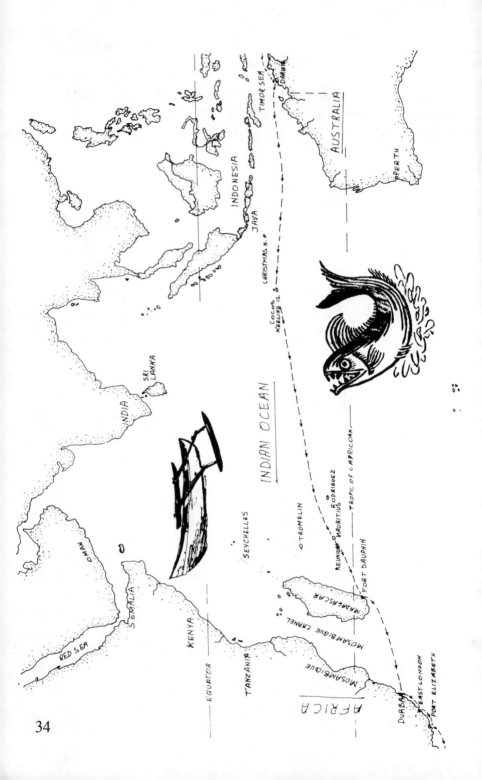

Chapter 3

CYCLONES

Acrohc was back in the water with a new coat of antifouling and packed full of food and fresh water. I went to the Darwin port officials and said, 'I would like clearance to leave with my yacht.'

'When?'

'Tomorrow, New Year's Eve. Is it possible?'

'Certainly. Is "that", the official asked, pointing to the papers, the size of the yacht?'

'Yes.'

'Twelve foot? Is that correct?'

'Yes, that's right,' I said.

'What's your next port of call?' he asked.

He'd got me there. 'Somewhere towards Africa, probably the Cocos Islands,' I replied vaguely.

Customs didn't even try to come on board to clear me. My boat wasn't large enough to smuggle anything big.

Early in the afternoon of New Year's Eve *Acrohc* was moored in the hot and windy harbour next to *Zitoon* and *Wave Dancer*. Both of these boats were crammed with well-wishers, including Daniel and Anne-Marie and the twins. Everyone had turned out to see me leave the harbour. I couldn't believe how many friends I'd made in such a short stay in Darwin. There was no shortage of bottles and we were all in a happy mood. There were many toasts to my trip, to *Acrohc*, to the New Year, to the sea etc. etc. My log book was signed by one and all and inscribed with wishes for good winds and an easy trip. It was time to leave. The weather broadcaster forecasted a storm at sea but I didn't care—I might as well get used to them.

The mooring lines were untied and *Acrohc* was off. We were accompanied for a short time by the two other yachts before everyone waved goodbye and turned to sail back to the harbour to continue the celebrations.

It was getting late and by the time I reached the open sea it was completely dark. All around me distant lightening lit up big black storm clouds. The wind grew stronger, lifting up the waves until *Acrohc* became uncomfortably playful. Then the forecast storm hit and *Acrohc* really came alive. I didn't expect the storm to last very long, as is usual in those waters, but this one lasted almost all of that first night.

After a month ashore it was easy to be seasick. The celebratory drinks didn't help and I was really sick—horribly sick. To add to my discomfort, the blankets I was sitting on were soaked with perspiration—it was so hot in the little cabin. As the lightening flashed I caught glimpses of a yacht heading into the harbour I had just left and I wondered who the lucky people were who would shortly be enjoying a cool shower and drink at the yacht club. Ahead of me lay 2,000 miles of sea; no showers and no cold beer for a long time.

At midnight I wrote in the log book for the first day of 1985, *Happy New Year, no celebrations because of the storm, seasick*. It wasn't that I'd stayed up especially to celebrate the New Year, it was simply that I was still close to land and I had to keep awake in case of a wind change. Nevertheless, I had to sleep sometime and after midnight, I took one hour naps. It was most uncomfortable, like trying to sleep in a bumper car, but I felt so sick that I even slept too well. When I woke in the morning the storm had vanished and I felt a lot better. In fact, I was well enough to open the bottle of New Year champagne.

The weather on the third day out of Darwin was good enough for me to start experimenting with the sextant, but my calculations were way out. I did everything according to the book but the result gave me a position 600 miles to the south compared to the R.D.F. Something was wrong. I suspected that my watch wasn't accurate enough for the calculations which have to be made to the exact second. I tried to pick up Greenwich Mean Time (GMT) on my little radio, but I couldn't find the right frequency. I tried a spot of fishing but didn't have any luck with that either.

That night another storm hit us. Off we went on another bumper car ride. Actually, *Acrohc* was better than a bumper car; she not only went forwards, backwards and from side to side, but she went up and down too.

The fourth day's log entry read: *Very good sailing, better at sextant, finally got GMT on short wave radio. Surprised at night by violent storm lasting three hours, sails often hit the water. 'Here we go again.'* This one was the most violent storm so far. Out in the open sea the waves were strong enough to knock *Acrohc* down. But at least I'd got over my seasickness and this seemed to make everything easier to cope with.

The following days saw us tackling persistent headwinds and the occasional calm.

January 8: Saw a fishing boat. This was what I'd been waiting for, a chance to use my new VHF radio for the first time. I wanted to get a position fix from the fishing boat to see how accurate my sextant readings were. Also, after eight days at sea, I was looking forward to a chat with someone. But, they didn't answer my call...maybe they didn't feel like chatting.

That night another of the short but annoying storms hit.

January 10: Happy, my sextant position matches the RDF signals! I was still getting clear signals from the Australian mainland.

January 11: Big tuna got away, lost three lures so far.

January 13: Strong winds in the night, lost one more lure.

January 16: Getting itchy skin on chest and stomach from rash. This rash, which was probably caused by the heat, was to last until I reached the Cocos Islands. I was spending most of the time in the cabin with the hatch closed. I had to keep it closed when going to windward, because every time *Acrohc* hit a wave the spray got in the cabin.

January 17: Lost one more lure and still no fish, serious trouble from salt wet sores, adding to the skin rash. I had developed small blisters on my skin. In a day or so they burst open leaving raw spots that would not heal because of the damp. They had first appeared on my bottom, back and elbows, areas where I was the most often wet, but they later spread all over my body and added to the discomfort I was already experiencing from the itchy rash.

January 18: A good day, storm gave us good winds for a while. That day I sighted another ship and this time had better luck contacting them with the radio. The ship was called *La Pampa* and was sailing for India. They asked me the size of my 'vessel' and my destination. When I told them I was going to Africa with a possible stop at Cocos there was a pause then, 'Rather you than me, mate.' An Australian crew! They offered assistance but all I needed was a position fix. I was pleased to find that it matched with the one I'd worked out using my sextant, only differing by 20 miles. This was good for a beginner but still left room for improvement. Later I often got readings accurate to within five miles.

Soon after the chat with *La Pampa* it rained and I got some calmer weather. When the rain started I was in such a rush to take a shower to sooth my skin that I tripped on the genoa sheet and found myself taking a bath instead. I quickly surfaced, but only to see *Acrohc's* stern already out of reach. Luckily, I always kept a long line trailing behind whenever I went on deck or went swimming for this very reason and boy I'm glad I did.

Headwinds continued with the occasional calm. Whenever it was calm I often dived over the side for a refreshing swim or to clean barnacles and weeds off *Acrohc's* bottom which accumulated despite the coat of antifouling. The 'undergrowth' could slow our speed considerably and had to be scrubbed off at least every two weeks.

The wet sores persisted mainly because I had nothing dry to lie on. I could dry out anything wet by hanging it out during the day in the sun, but at night things quickly became wet again as the salt in them absorbed the humidity in the cabin.

January 27: Backache giving me problems, exercising 10 min. daily but humidity doesn't help. Two hours of rainstorm but could not collect water as too violent. 'Ghost' ship passed 500 metres away but didn't answer radio calls, would have been good to have a chat.

January 29: Another thirty minute storm. These tropical storms with winds of up to 40 or 50 knots could pop up from nowhere and disappear just as fast. They weren't so bad during the day when I could see the dark clouds coming and could prepare for it, but at night they were a problem.

January 30: Stormy all day. I saw the 'ghost' ship again that day and still couldn't get radio contact. It was heading across my path but suddenly turned north. I saw that it was a Japanese long-line fishing boat and its crew was busy setting lines. The fact that it was a fishing boat probably accounted for its zigzagging. (It was only much later that I learned they are not equipped with VHF radios.)

Later that day I came upon another ship, *Stanlock*. This time I got a position check from them which almost matched mine—only 10 miles difference! They also radioed a message back to my family who, I was sure, would be starting to worry about my whereabouts.

January 31: Storms continue. I started to realize that I should have installed more vents but I hadn't anticipated that it would be so hot. In fact, that night it was calm but so hot that I couldn't resist sleeping with the hatch open. It was lovely and I slept so well that I didn't feel the approaching storm coming until too late.

Acrohc caught the storm under full sail resulting in a 'knockdown' which is when the mast hits the sea. I awoke to pots and pans falling all over me and water coming into the cabin. The surprise was such that I didn't know whether to close the hatch first or reduce sail but managed to do both roughly at the same time by releasing the winch for the headsail sheet with my left hand and closing the hatch with the right! The mast came out of the water and *Acrohc* righted herself a little.

It was not a nice way to wake up. A lot of water had got in, drenching the already damp mess inside. There was water sloshing around in my bed and I had to wring the blankets out before trying to sleep again. Luckily the foam mattress which had got a soaking had a vinyl cover.

February 1: Saw another ship which didn't want to talk to me.

Two days later *Acrohc* had reached the point on the pilot chart that showed good and continuing easterly winds so I anticipated a good run from there on. I was halfway to the Cocos Islands, only a thousand miles to go. To celebrate, I opened a bottle of wine given to me in Darwin for just this occasion and then rounded the meal off with some whiskey. (The bottle was low when the storm hit that night. I don't remember much of what happened but the log reads, *Violent storm, no problems.*)

*****

I had reached 'the point of no return'—the point from where I knew I wouldn't be tempted to give up and I knew there would be favourable winds from there on.

The pilot chart was right. Slowly the headwind turned around and, with good easterly winds blowing, I hoped to make Cocos in about two weeks. The waves had stopped splashing water over *Acrohc* and I could keep either the hatch or at least one of the cabin's portholes open most of the time. My morale improved as did the wet sores. My skin felt a lot better generally. We were now averaging 75 miles a day.

February 5: 37 days at sea. That morning I busied myself setting up a trawling line with a new lure after losing yet another one to a fish that was probably too big for it. Everything was going smoothly. The pilot fish was still escorting us, the sky was clear and I was starting to enjoy the now reasonable well-behaved waves. The nice thing about the waves, apart from the smoothness of the swell, was that they were going in the same direction as us and at about the same speed; we were literally riding them. *Acrohc's* only movement was a gentle up and down motion with a slight increase of speed as she rose and rode each wave. In between waves she would return to her normal speed of three knots.

I relaxed, watching the yellow and black striped pilot fish darting through the water, but still on the look out for something larger to catch. Then I spotted a large, dark shadow tailing us just below the surface. It was too big for my line but, curiosity aroused, I stood on my seat for a better look and recognised the outline of a Hammerhead shark. It cruised back and forth behind us probably stalking my pilot fish. I decided not to cast the trawling line until it left—not that I wouldn't eat shark but one longer than the boat was just too big.

February 12: All is well, days going by nicely.

I was starting to pick up clear radio signals from the Cocos Islands and was happy to know that I was on course. At the rate I was going all I had to do was sail straight ahead for five more days—only five more days to a shower and a cold beer! I slept well that night.

The following morning, I discovered that the wind's direction had changed by a few degrees to the beam. By now, it was coming from the north and its considerably increased force meant I had to close the hatch again. That evening with the wind coming directly from the west I watched the waves through the porthole.

Just before dark the self steering cables gave way and I had to replace them while *Acrohc* wandered on her own chosen course. Mission accomplished, I fell asleep confident that this storm would pass during the night like all the others had. How wrong I was.

I was greeted in the morning, after spending a restless night, by a white sea with spray flying from the crests of the breaking waves.

They weren't lifting very high as the strong wind kept flattening them but they were moving at an incredible speed. By looking at the sea's condition I estimated that the wind was blowing at over 60 knots.

The wind made a cacophony of noises. Normally a strong wind whistles through the rigging but this one went past that point and howled through the rigging and sails and whooshed through the air vent as though annoyed by finding *Acrohc* in its path. The sound of the waves crashing and hammering against the hull added to the chaos. Altogether it was hell.

I argued with the wind, 'No it's not right, you've got to blow from the other side—it says so in the pilot chart.' But the conditions worsened throughout the night and the next day. I couldn't understand why this storm was lasting for so long. I wasn't sure but I felt that this just had to be a cyclone.

The three days of continuous storm, classified in my log as '*very violent*' were enough to reduce my skin to its worst condition yet. Everything was soaking wet including me, not only from the spray getting in through the small gap that I often left in the hatchway but also from condensation and my perspiration. Despite the strong winds outside, it was still terribly hot inside the cabin.

At night it wasn't so hot but I still couldn't sleep for all the noise. That night I heard someone calling my name. Was I hearing voices or was there another boat nearby? I looked around in the dark but couldn't see anything. I tried to go back to sleep but again and again I heard the voices calling. I knew I was only hallucinating but it sounded so real that I couldn't ignore it. I'd been told by other yachties that this could happen and that it was caused by extreme tiredness. To a tired mind squeaking noises can easily sound like a known voice. I often had to check, just in case there was someone there. It happened on many nights and sometimes even during the day.

The conditions hadn't changed by the morning of February 16 then all of a sudden the wind started to die down. By eleven o'clock there was hardly a breeze and the radical waves disappeared altogether. I didn't know which Saint to thank. It was so peaceful. The gentle rocking of *Acrohc* made it hard to believe that only a moment ago it was hell. I started thinking clearly again and as soon as I could, I put all the blankets out to dry. Then I made myself a cup of coffee and really enjoyed it while sitting on the open hatch. To my surprise the pilot fish was still with us.

I had hoped that the winds from the east would come back as the pilot chart said they should at that time of year, but my blankets weren't even dry when, just after noon, the headwinds came back. Before long I was faced with what seemed to be the same white sea, the speeding waves and the hellish noise. I hoped that it would be a passing squall but it went on through the night and continued the following day without respite. As time passed I had to admit to myself that this one too wasn't a squall. It prevented me from using the spirit stove again so it was back to a diet of biscuits, cold baked bean salad and no coffee!

The next day brought the same hell. I had now had six days of misery with only a two hour break. If I hadn't been so close to Cocos, I would have literally 'Gone with the Wind' and headed south to Mauritius, 2,500 miles away. I constantly had to fight this urge as I was only making ten miles a day and had no idea how long the headwinds would last.

But just before noon on the next day, February 19 (the 51st day of the leg), the weather eased. I opened the hatch as soon as the waves settled a bit and, to the southeast, I saw clouds in a strange circular formation; the centre of the depression that I thought might be the eye of a cyclone. I got a sextant fix at noon and found my position to be only 140 miles from Cocos.

The winds soon started blowing again, getting worse as the days wore on and I couldn't make any sense of the weather. I should have realised that it was cyclonic but I had been told that when a cyclone passes overhead the wind changes direction. This wind was blowing almost constantly from the west so I didn't believe it was a cyclone.

It was difficult to do anything. Even opening a tin of food was a problem because it takes two hands and I had to hold on to something all the time. I had wrapped up every glass jar to prevent breakages and this was a success but a two litre plastic bottle of vinegar didn't resist the constant jarring and broke open. All the tins of food were sprayed with vinegar and started to corrode. The food locker was an absolute mess.

It kept blowing day and night with waves crashing into *Acrohc* like runaway trucks. To sleep, I pulled the chart table over me to reduce the space in the cabin so I wouldn't be thrown about so much. I managed to take short naps, learning to sleep while holding on to something, but I had to turn often because of the painful wet sores. The only place where there were no sores was my chest but even this was covered in the horrible itchy rash which was continuing to irritate me and which worsened on hot days.

Sometimes, just to get some relief from the heat I left the cabin and crouched on the deck, hanging on to the mast. The spray from the waves refreshed me a little but I couldn't stay on deck for very long periods of time. Under normal conditions it was safe enough on deck because there was always something to hang on to, but in this weather hanging on to something was too difficult and I could only manage it for about ten minutes at a time. And although I shut the hatch as quickly as possible going in and out of the cabin, a lot of water found its way in.

The relief I felt from my trips on deck was only temporary. After being back inside for only a few minutes I couldn't sit or lie down. Sometimes I knelt or squatted but as I had to hold on to the side of the cabin all the time it was too tiring. I was constantly moving around tying to find a better position. If only I'd had something dry to sit on! I couldn't write long notes in my log but I did manage to pen quite a few nasty insults directed mostly to the sea gods.

All things considered my morale had been good but I was now getting depressed and frustrated that I could do nothing to improve my situation. It was February 25th, 57 days since starting out from Darwin and 12 days since all hell had broken loose. I was getting closer to Cocos and I was trying to keep a look out for land. Every time I saw a dark shape on the horizon my hopes rose but each time it turned out to be just another cloud. (A low lying cloud can look exactly like an island from a distance.)

I began to wonder if Cocos was really where I believed it to be. Could my calculations be wrong? I was supposed to be only ten miles from the islands and I should have been able to see them. I wondered how much more I could take before I snapped and went completely nuts.

The following morning the wind eased once more and as soon as it was calm enough I tried to dry a few things before the return of the wind. I also had a swim and wondered if the crazy weather had finished with me.

When I climbed aboard again I checked the horizon for land and saw another large dark shape. To get a better look I climbed up on the boom. This cloud looked definitely different. It seemed to be

Cocos Keeling Islands, at last after the cyclones

darker, with more defined lines, but I still couldn't be sure. I went on with my chores of drying clothes and blankets, at the same time keeping an eye on the 'cloud'. After breakfast it was still there so I climbed onto the boom again. This time I could see it was definitely not a cloud. It was land. It was the Cocos Islands!

I can't say how excited I felt when I was gradually able to distinguish the tops of coconut trees, the white surf, sand and then green vegetation. I could hardly believe it was real. I was so happy that I jumped up and down on the seat and if the deck had been bigger I'd have danced on it.

Fifty-eight days had passed since I left Darwin. I was desperate for a cold beer and a shower and to be able to wash out all the clothing, blankets and pillows, all of which were stiff with salt. I was longing for fresh vegetables and I couldn't wait to eat an entire lettuce! I realised that, strangely, all I had been missing were the material things and not human company at all; I couldn't understand it. To think that after 58 days of hearing only imaginary voices I'd want to stop only for a cold beer and a lettuce, despite the fact that there were bound to be some pretty girls on the island. This peculiar attitude must have developed as I unconsciously conditioned myself to being alone. But this was going too far. Thanks to the lettuce I snapped out of it.

I motored towards the islands, calling up the authorities by VHF. They said they'd come to see me about clearance in the morning and told me to anchor for the night north of the island group in the shelter of Direction Island. I told them that *Acrohc* was a 12 foot yacht, but they seemed unable to grasp that fact and kept referring to her as 12 metres.

After dark, I anchored where instructed. It was peaceful and the water was clear. When I dropped the anchor, a huge manta ray glided up and cruised around *Acrohc*. It may have been that it was attracted by my navigation light, but I know it came to say 'Welcome!'

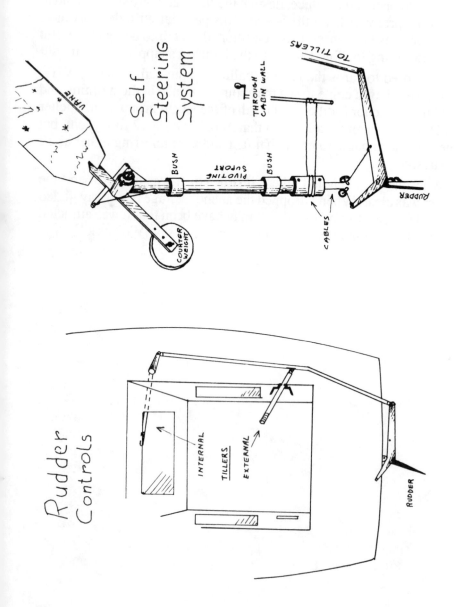

Self Steering System

VANE

THROUGH CABIN WALL

TO TILLERS

BUSH

PIVOTING SUPORT

BUSH

CABLES

RUDDER

COUNTER WEIGHT

Rudder Controls

INTERNAL

TILLERS

EXTERNAL

RUDDER

Chapter 4

ISLAND VOYAGING

The next morning, still anchored off Direction Island, I was awoken by the sound of a motor launch. It was circling as though it was searching for something. When they finally approached me they shouted across, 'We weren't looking for something this small. We were told it was a 12 metre yacht.'

The quarantine man refused to come aboard *Acrohc*. He had a strange look on his face. He was on the bow of the launch holding his brief case ready to jump onto the newly arrived yacht as he always did. But he was puzzled about where he should jump. He decided that I should meet him on the jetty, five kilometres away across the lagoon, at West Island.

The paperwork completed, he offered to show me around. As we drove through the coconut tree jungle to the Australian settlement, a village of about 250 people in the centre of the island, he couldn't stop asking questions. He was amazed that *Acrohc* had come through from Darwin. 'How did you manage in the cyclones?' he asked.

'Cyclones? I thought the wind was a bit strong,' I replied.

'Four of them. They came right through these islands and went in an easterly direction. Look at the broken trees,' he said as we passed the remains of some of the island's tallest trees that had been caught by the winds. *Acrohc* and I had survived the worst weather I'd imagined we'd have to encounter. The cyclones had passed right over us.

Acrohc's design had been put to the test and had come through with flying colours. Nothing had broken except the windvane cables. We hadn't even lost the mast, the least I'd expected would happen if we met a cyclone. I'd cursed her deep draft each time I'd run aground on the Queensland coast but thanks to it we hadn't capsized once. For a yacht only 12 feet long she couldn't have done any better. I was proud of my little boat . . . she was a real yacht! Her skipper might be a bit of a nut, but we'd done alright.

*****

In the right season there are usually many yachts anchored at the Cocos Keeling Islands, which are part of Australia, but I was the only one there at that time. Maybe that's why I got such good treatment from the locals. They even let me anchor next to the jetty on West Island when ordinarily visiting yachts have to anchor off Direction Island. West Island is one of the main islands in the small Cocos group. The islands surround a lagoon and cover an area of about ten square kilometres.

Everyone who came to look at *Acrohc* had the same thing to say, 'Sailing on a boat that small, and out of season, you've got to be crazy!' But they were all friendly and allowed me to use the facilities there. Most appreciated were the washing machines and I was able to wash the salt out of my clothing and blankets for the first time in eight weeks.

My itchy rash started to disappear and the 340 wet sores that I'd counted all over my body just before reaching the islands started to heal.

I spent the three week stay on the islands chatting, drinking and learning to walk again. I was a bit wobbly when I took my first steps ashore and, for a while, wasn't able to walk for very long because I had to build up my leg muscles again after so long at sea.

One day I visited Home Island across the lagoon. It has a population of 300, all of Malaysian descent. Their forefathers had been brought to the islands to work on coconut plantations. They had kept many of their customs and their language, but were losing the art of building their beautiful sailing boats or 'Jukong'. I saw many of these wooden boats on the beach at Home Island, all maintained meticulously, but I never saw one in the water; alloy boats were replacing them.

The island's inhabitants live in a very close community—a few work on West Island for the Australian government but hardly anyone has travelled beyond the Cocos group itself. I was invited to visit the primary school and talk to the children. They couldn't stop asking questions about my trip and the outside world and I did my best to satisfy their curiosity. I really enjoyed my day with them, learning a lot about their lifestyle. We kept in touch from then on and in one of their letters I found a small poem that I'll always remember:

> *Birds fly high,*
> *hard to catch.*
> *Sailors like you,*
> *hard to forget.*

The mail was slow to reach the Cocos Islands as there was only one plane a week. I wrote home while I was there and received a reply three week's later containing good news. An Australian magazine was interested in the story of my voyage so I started writing regularly for them. The extra money would come in handy and would take the pressure off my brother Henry who had promised to keep me 'afloat' if my savings didn't last the circumnavigation. He and my sister-in-law, Francesca, also took care of my paperwork which included sending on stories and photographs to various magazines. The trip would have been much harder without this backup.

I was never too worried about money for the trip as I knew my family wouldn't let me down if I ever became really strapped for cash. I could have found work en route as I had experience in boat building and other trades but I was afraid that stopping for work would make the whole trip too long and tempt me to give up.

*****

Relaxing on the islands was all very nice, but my skin had almost healed and the winds were right; it was time to go.

During my last week on the islands an extremely big cyclone had approached the area but it had passed somewhere to the south with only its tail catching the islands. The strong winds had tossed *Acrohc* violently at her anchorage, however when I left on the 14th of March the wind was really gentle and from the east, promising a 'holiday' trip to Mauritius. Of course, with 2,400 miles to go anything could happen.

I was still recovering from the farewell party and my feet were sore and swollen from all the walking I'd done, but the sailing was nice and I enjoyed being underway again.

For the first four days I managed only 45 miles a day so I had plenty of spare time on my hands. I tried fishing and nearly caught a dorado, but the hook didn't hold. I also saw a ship and it turned out to be the only one I'd see on this leg of the trip.

The fifth day's entry in the log reads, *Steadily increasing winds, no sleep, too rocky. Acrohc* always rocked a lot with running winds and as I was thrown from side to side in the cabin this made sleep difficult.

Day 6: Same strong winds, sunny, no sleep.

Day 8: Winds eased a little in morning, windvane cable broke again, repaired it, strong winds back before noon.

On the ninth day, March 22, the rough weather continued and I was starting to feel the effects of lost sleep. I heard lots of roosters and chickens on top of the usual dogs and children. I badly needed some sleep. My consolation was that we were going very fast and covering over 100 miles a day. That night the strong winds broke the cable on my windvane again.

Day 10: A little calmer, changed cable for nylon rope, got position fix. The past six days it had been impossible to take a position. Sometimes I could take sextant shots in spite of rough weather providing there were no big waves or swell. Being so small, *Acrohc* was lower in the water than most boats and the arc of the horizon was closer to me than it would have been on a larger boat. Also the line of the horizon could easily be distorted by the swell, which would give false readings.

Day 11: Strong winds make good sailing.

Day 12: Oiled tins rusted by broken vinegar bottle, lost breakfast bowl when washing it over the side.

Day 13: Strong winds persist, make it uncomfortable and hard to sleep.

On the 14th night, the smell of something very fishy woke me. With a torch I searched the deck to try to find the source of the smell. Dead flying fish often met their doom on the deck as when trying to escape predators they take to the air and I usually had to clear the deck of several every morning. This time however the smell was such that I couldn't wait 'til morning.

But back in the cabin and mission accomplished the smell was still there strong. Searching again, I finally spotted one wedged inside the dorado vent. The boat's constant rolling made the operation a bit tricky but I finally got it out by using a piece of wire fashioned into a hook.

I often spent hours at a time watching schools of flying fish. In calm weather they are easy prey but in the right conditions they take to the air to hopefully elude their predators. They always surface against the wind as they need this headwind to takeoff. They flap their tails while still in the water, increasing their speed enough to get airborne. Once in the air they turn on their sides and glide for 200 metres or more before hitting the water again. Of course, there is always the danger of a seabird swooping in for the kill when they're in mid air. A flying fish's lot is not a happy one!

Day 15: Good going, halfway to Mauritius! Nice purple coloured sunset. Usual rough day. Stormy night.

Day 17: Lost cushion when trying to dry it on rigging, still can't take sight.

Day 18: Sunday, good position, about 850 miles from Mauritius.

Day 19: Good sailing, moderate winds, faint radio beacon signal from Mauritius, wet sores are starting again.

Day 21: Usual fast going, hard to sleep, difficult to cook but still able to make coffee.

Day 23: Happy Birthday Mum. I used dates like birthdays to break the monotony of the days. Good old Mum. I wondered what she was up to. I imagined her gardening and taking care of the strawberry patch she is so fond of. Every time I visit her she makes sure I get a good helping of strawberries. I knew she'd be worried sick about me, perhaps giving up hope that I'd get back alive. I felt guilty putting her through such an ordeal of worry but I couldn't help it. I would have really pleased Mum if I'd have taken a nice steady job, perhaps married and bought a house and, particularly, kept away from the sea. Much as I feel guilty I don't think I'll ever be able to settle down.

Day 24: Easter Friday, got position sight—21°33' South, 65°38' West—then wind came back hard, 3 to 4 metre waves by evening. Passed Rodrigues Island. I would have liked to have called at the island for a break but I had been told that the entrance to the anchorage was very shallow. So, as I didn't want to run in to it during the night, I kept a good 100 miles away from it.

Day 25: Same weather, finally got good radio signal, violent night.

Day 27: Weather repeat, plus storm in the morning, no fix. Had a wash on deck. Starting to get bored. Ninety percent of my time was now spent inside the cabin! I was also worried about how close I was to Mauritius. Because of the weather I just could not get sextant shots and the RDF only told me my direction.

Day 28: Same weather, can't be far now.

Day 29: Land in sight at 15h22! Position nearly as calculated by sextant at noon, latitude was good, longitude 5 miles out. Good weather too.

I arrived on the southern side of the island of Mauritius after dark. My destination was Port Louis on the western side of the island but as it was dark I decided to head out to sea for the night so that I could get some badly needed sleep. Next morning I discovered that I was a bit too far south and it took me all day to get back to the island.

As I sailed along the shoreline admiring the many resorts where people were having fun on the beach I couldn't help wondering just why I was putting myself through such an ordeal. Eight weeks of misery to Cocos followed by another four weeks of just as miserable conditions to reach Mauritius. Did I really need the sleepless nights, the days without a proper meal, the constant rolling and rocking? The loneliness wasn't a problem, but the monotony of the days was. But despite it all, I had no regrets and no second thoughts about continuing on; I wanted to get that record. Mind you, the standing record for the circumnavigation was for a boat measuring 18 feet 4 inches and to qualify I could have built a boat just two inches smaller—why on earth had I built one six feet smaller?!

Some years previously I had built a 33 foot sloop to sail around the world. She would have been perfect for the job. But six months after her launching I realised that I wouldn't be able to afford all of the necessary equipment and the travelling costs without working along the way...not really my idea of cruising. It shattered my dreams but I had to sell her.

I used the money from her sale to start a boat building business in partnership with Henry, hoping that this would eventually provide enough money to realise my dream. Business started off slowly but after a year we were doing well and getting a good reputation. But my dream of cruising was still far from being realised and I started getting restless. It looked like being ten years before I could get away, so the idea of building and fitting out a 12 foot boat became more and more attractive.

One day I was looking at my 12 foot dinghy and thought to myself that if I really wanted to go cruising why did I need to have a big boat when I could fit everything necessary into a 12 foot boat? The idea became more attractive as I realised that a 12 foot boat was affordable and would leave me with money left over to travel with. So, in my spare time I built my little one. When I was ready to leave, my other brother, John, took over for me at the boatyard so that I was really free to wander.

LITTLE PIED CORMORANT

I spent the day motoring back to the island, approaching the harbour around midnight. The harbour lights were difficult to pick out as they blended in with the lights of the city in the background. I felt a bump and just to carry on with good habits, we ran aground. I threw out the anchor, put the kerosene light on deck and went to bed, knowing that it was useless to try anything further. After all, one more night after a month at sea wasn't going to make any difference.

When morning came I found that we were actually in the channel, perhaps just a touch close to the edge of it, but I got off the coral easily and motored towards the harbour, tying up at last alongside other yachts at the Customs jetty.

This was a strange country for me. I new nothing about it except that it used to be a French colony, but some of the fishermen I'd met on the way into the harbour didn't understand French and I'd had even less luck with English. Most of the population were of Indian descent but there were many Africans and Chinese with some whites making up the balance.

I discovered that the official languages were English and French. Indian was also widely spoken but the most common was Creole. Creole sounded to me like a mixture of old French, English and Portuguese. (The Portuguese influence came from passing pirates in the 1700's.) As I was born in France I speak French, so after a few days I could understand Creole fairly well. Trying to speak it though was fun and a good way of mixing with the welcoming locals.

The island was beautiful, both green and mountainous, and was once the home of the Dodo, a wingless bird now extinct because it was so easy to catch. (I was told that they looked something like a chicken but bigger and stockier.)

There were many comfortable anchorages in the clear waters of the coast. I stayed a week in Grand Bay where I tied *Acrohc* to the swimming pool wall of a hotel. It took only a small jump from *Acrohc* to a terraced area where I could enjoy morning coffee with my new-found friends—what a way to start a day.

From Grand Bay I moved 'just around the corner' to Peribere, a smaller bay lined with a golden beach. I anchored there for a week. Each night a group of young locals and yachties met on the beach and sat around a fire, eating grilled fish, drinking beer and playing folk songs. One or two guitars and a drum was all they needed to create the atmosphere—if there was no drum a steel jerrycan did the job. The nights were warm and the parties often went on until the early hours.

Among the new friends I made was Tonga Bill. When we first met he was struck by the size of *Acrohc* and, in fact, he was cruising in a boat like the one that held the record I was after. But he wasn't after any record and was happy to make a living from his wood, ivory, coral and sharks' teeth carvings. As a souvenir he carved a Polynesian story about the sea on *Acrohc's* bowsprit, the only timber on her. (When I reached the Kingdom of Tonga much later in my trip, I found that he was somewhat of a celebrity there as he was the only Tongan in 'modern days' to have built a yacht and gone cruising.)

I would have liked to have stayed longer on Mauritius but the girls were too friendly! If I wanted to stay single and complete the trip I would have to leave. Anyway, three weeks was enough of a rest for the next leg to Reunion Island, only 120 miles away.

*****

The trip to Reunion was an easy sail with light headwinds and calm nights which let me get good night's sleep with the hatch open. At night the sky was beautiful and clear, brightened by the Milky Way and infinite stars. It seemed almost a shame to sleep and I'd lie on my bunk for hours watching for falling stars and satellites, which were easy to pick out in the clean air. Each satellite took about 10 minutes to move across the sky.

On only my second day out of Mauritius I could see the lower part of my new island under its huge cloud. Mountainous islands such as Reunion are almost always capped with a big cloud caused by the temperature difference. Sometimes these clouds entirely hide the islands and despite the constant wind they are not blown away because they continually reform.

That night I was disturbed only by a large shark. The sound of its fin through the calm water made me get up. By torchlight I saw it swimming hurriedly around and under *Acrohc* as though chasing some small prey that had probably sought refuge under *Acrohc's* hull.

After one more night off the rugged shore, spent somewhat more vigilantly than the previous one, I entered the harbour of Saint Pierre. A strong following wind had come up and we almost surfed in. The locals told me later that when they had seen the small sail in the distance they said, 'There goes another stupid windsurfer we'll have to rescue!'

When we got into the harbour a yachtie showed me where to find a free mooring. He also insisted on lending me his dinghy. Philippe's dinghy came in very handy as I often had trouble keeping my plastic inflatable dinghy afloat. It was really only a toy, not a tender, but it was all I could store and often the only way I could get ashore if I couldn't get a lift with someone else. A few times I swam ashore as an alternative, taking dry clothes with me in a plastic bag. This, of course, wasn't always possible.

Chapter 5

FIRE ON BOARD

Reunion is a French island which was used as a base by pirates in the late 17th century. Its inhabitants still use a Creole dialect not unlike that spoken on Mauritius. A lot more of the old expressions and old nautical terms have been kept though. I heard many tales about buried treasure and famous pirates and, in fact, some of the inhabitants are descendants of pirates. The majority of the population though are of French, African and Indian descent.

I happened to be there in May when the streets were alive with the bright colours of the Tamil ceremonies. One day I watched a parade making its way to the beach. The women wore vividly coloured dresses while the men's bare chests were covered with painted markings. Once on the beach some of the men performed a ceremony that involved piercing their skin with long needles...without seeming to feel any pain. It was a pity that I missed the fire walking ceremony which I had been told was really something to see.

On Reunion, the city peoples' way of life and standard of living are comparable to the south of France. However, there are other inhabitants called 'little whites'—white settlers who took refuge in the higher regions of the island during the slave revolts of long ago. Some of these 'refugees' built villages in small and isolated valleys and never returned to the coastal settlements. Their villages were discovered only recently and their lifestyle was likened to that of the people of the Stone Age. Mind you, after visiting one of the villages I understood their reluctance to rejoin 'civilisation'.

Tonga Bill's fiancee, Christine, was working on Reunion and she offered to take me up to Grand Bassin, one of the most recently discovered settlements. I caught my first sight of the village from a lookout 1,000 metres above it. It was tightly wedged in a little valley between mountains some 2,000 metres high. It wasn't easy to get there, the track consisting mainly of roughly hewn steps cut into the steep mountainside, but the four kilometre walk down was fun and led to some of the most enchanting country I'd ever seen. The vegetation was dense and green and was only relieved by little tracks that connected the wooden or stone cottages. And there was a river which tumbled over a fall to a crystal clear perfect swimming pond. A world of no motors and no electricity—it was like stepping back in time.

When we arrived in the village itself I was amazed by the serenity. We asked the way to the waterfall and there ate lunch in a 'Garden of Eden'. After our picnic we returned to the village and chatted to some of the villagers who were repairing one of the houses. I learned that despite a shortage of 'mod cons' they lived as well as anyone in the 20th century enjoying, in fact, an easier and happier way of life than most.

The trip back up the mountainside was another story. Even Fidor the dog accompanying us had trouble. I was told that some of the villagers make the trip three or four times a week to sell their produce in town. I was glad to only do it once.

I didn't go on a walk up to the live volcano because its summit was often in the clouds. It would have been a cold trip and useless because of poor visibility. Besides, I would've had to get up early to make the trip—a difficult thing to do after all the late nights. I wasn't to blame though; everyone kept calling on me to eat, drink and be merry, and the French-Creole food . . . 'ou la la'!

I loved the curried lobster served by the small restaurant on the waterfront (the owner dived for them himself). Then there was the yachtie who provided me with a lavish free meal at his restaurant, just because I fixed a motor for him. Then two yachts I'd met at Mauritius arrived, more reasons to have that drink or go out to the disco or that little cafe that stayed open late . . .

Reunion remains one of the nicest placed I visited. I could have easily stayed for more than three weeks. The French pastry alone could have kept me there longer.

*****

The day of departure came and I went to the police station for clearance. They stamped my passport and said, 'Bon voyage', the extent of the formalities on Reunion.

It was best to leave Reunion at around midnight at high tide when the wind stopped rolling the waves towards the entrance of the harbour but by the time I actually got away it was 1:30 on a Friday morning. I was not superstitious though and always left simply when I was ready. Besides, Madagascar, the wild island, was waiting.

Outside the harbour a strong south easterly wind was waiting for me and it lasted all that night and the following day. The third day however found us almost becalmed with a storm heading for us. But luckily, although it circled us it eventually backtracked so I was able to get a good night's sleep.

The next day the weather and water were still calm and as a result *Acrohc* was only moving at one knot—the perfect time to make pancakes I thought. I mixed the dough, adding milk and egg, and ate each one as it came off the stove. They were really nice.

The spirit in the stove started to run out and I needed to refill it to keep on cooking. I should have turned the stove off but knowing that the burner would then get cold and have to be warmed up before I could relight it, I poured the spirit into the stove using a little spout I'd made for precisely this purpose. I'd done it many times before but this time a wave hit *Acrohc* just as I was pouring and I spilled a little of the alcohol. In a split second I saw the stove's flame get to the spill, leap up through the spout and into the bottle. There was a dull 'WHOOMP' and the full bottle exploded in my hands throwing flaming alcohol all over the cabin and me.

Luckily the hatch was open, for as I flew out of the cabin to jump into the water, I heard rather than felt the crackle of my beard on fire. By reflex I jumped towards the bow and how I ever got out and through the rigging so fast I'll never know. And even as I dived overboard, I was turning in the water to surface and grab onto the side of the deck so that I could climb back on. It was normally a bit of a struggle to heave myself back on deck after a dip, but this time I achieved it in record time.

As I got back on board, I saw the flames pouring from the hatchway and I didn't think twice about trying to save my boat as, wet enough to withstand the flames, I dived through the hatchway to grab the extinguisher that was in the cabin.

The extinguisher was attached to the side of the cabin by a simple fastener, but the tenth of a second it took to release seemed a long time—so long, in fact, that in that fleeting moment I recalled the story of a friend who, after a plane crash, could not unfasten the safety belt because of panic.

I clearly remember telling myself not to panic, undo the bracket, lift the handle and then strike the top. I hit the top of the extinguisher a little too hard and it nearly flew out of my hands but I held on to it and sprayed the cabin. It didn't take long to put the fire out but as there was still a lot of smoke I sprayed a second time just to be sure. Then the full realisation of what had happened hit me.

I started to feel the pain, the smell of burnt plastic and the sight of the cabin seeming to add to it. Everything seemed either blackened from the fire or white from the extinguisher powder. There was pancake dough, sprayed by the exploding bottle, all over the place. I was wet, cold and hot all at the same time. I couldn't go inside because it was still too hot in there. I was freezing despite my burnt skin.

I remember asking myself if I'd done the right thing by diving into the sea. A second more in the fire and it would have been all over. The pain now was horrible. I couldn't even get inside to dry myself. I wanted to lie down but I couldn't sit on the open hatch because of the heat. So, I stood on the foredeck where the heat of the fire hadn't reached, trying to think of what to do next.

Some time later (I have no idea how long) the cabin had cooled down enough for me to pop down and grab a towel and burn cream. I then stretched a sun shade over the boat. The strange hot-cold sensation had left me but I still knew I had to keep the sun off. I smothered myself in the cream, using the entire tube. My chest wasn't

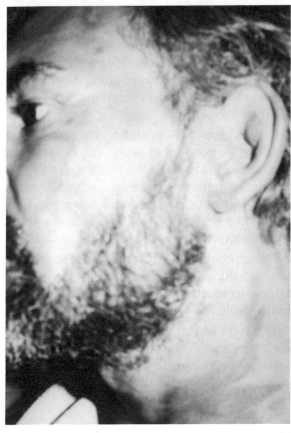

Burns to the face, after the fire

burnt thanks to a T-shirt and I had been wearing underwear, but my legs, arms and face were in a bad way.

I looked like a plucked and half cooked chicken. I had no body hair left, half of my beard was gone as was some of the hair on the left side of my head. My left ear was burnt. So were my nose and neck—the latter hurting the most. Even my feet were burnt.

For the first time I thought about turning on the distress beacon but I wondered what anyone could do for me. Probably they'd give me cream and painkillers, both of which I had and had by then used. If I called for rescue, help wouldn't arrive for a day or two if I was lucky, and besides, they would have taken me off *Acrohc* and left her behind.

I couldn't leave her after damaging her so much already. Most of the lining of the cabin was gone; everything plastic on the galley side had been burnt. The compass glass had bubbled, one of the water pumps was bent, the central foam cushion had a hole in it the size of a plate, bits of blanket were gone, the front laminated glass porthole had cracked and almost everything was covered with white powder. What a mess!

I lay on the bunk, spending the rest of that day trying to find a comfortable position to lie in. The next morning the pain wasn't so intense but the mess in the cabin was still there and I couldn't find the energy to start the clean up. The wind started to blow a bit stronger and *Acrohc's* rocking made me rub my burns on the bunk. We kept sailing in a westerly direction. I wasn't worrying about our position and I simply wasn't up to using the sextant.

Things continued much the same for the next couple of days, then some of the blisters burst and the raw surfaces they left were too painful to touch. I stayed in bed day and night just trying to keep comfortable.

The sixth day after the fire was no different except that I had to keep watch for land. I hoped to sight a ship too so I could ask for a position fix. I estimated that I was still far enough from land to relax that day and the pain from the slowly healing wounds seemed a little better.

With the pain easing I started to realise how close to death I'd come and just how stupid I'd been. I had no one to blame but myself for the situation and I got an idea of why so many sailors prefer to sail solo; had someone else caused the fire I'd have thrown him overboard.

To err is human but at sea there is no room for error. I had made a mistake which had nearly cost my life but I had learned another valuable lesson.

I was looking forward to being able to sleep without the movement that caused the rubbing of my wounds, and on the seventh day after the fire, I knew we would be nearing land but I couldn't see the sun to get a fix. My destination was Fort Dauphin and I'd been heading for 30 miles north of it to allow for the strong current that ran down the coast. Later that day I sighted Madagascar and discovered that I'd overestimated the current's strength; I was 20 miles too far north. I was then becalmed five miles from land!

Motoring for the rest of the day back down the coast, we finally entered the bay of Fort Dauphin late that night.

I had cleaned up some of the mess and only some of the raw patches hadn't healed. It had been a ten day trip as I'd planned. There had been a hiccup along the way, but in the end I got there.

Of course I never left on a Friday again!

I anchored outside the harbour and slept as I'd never slept before, not waking until late the next morning.

I hadn't been able to get a visa for Madagascar before leaving Reunion so I wanted to contact the authorities before I entered the harbour. I tried raising the Port Captain on the VHF radio for ages without success. (I learned later that he didn't have one.) While I was still trying though, a few dugout canoes passed by looking as though they were on their way home after a fishing trip. Madagascar used to be a French colony so I tried talking to them in French but all they

did was smile back at me. One of them knew two words, 'du pain'.
He was asking me for bread! Where would I get bread after ten days
at sea?! I would have given them some food but I wanted to get entry
clearance first; I didn't want any trouble with the authorities.

I gave up on the radio and decided to enter the harbour. When I
neared the quay I was told not to dock and to wait for the police. Half
an hour later they showed up and I was allowed to tie up. The police,
however, didn't come alone. They seemed to have been joined by
every official in the town and some soldiers in full combat uniforms.
I started to get a bit worried. Did they think I was a terrorist or
something?

At first they treated me like one. I was taken to a small Customs
office which was jam packed with everyone who could fit in.
Everyone was asking questions and taking notes. It was a bit comical
and I could hear, 'He's wounded' and 'Let me through. I'm from the
insurance.' Most of them spoke Malgash and I couldn't understand
very much of it. After an hour in the little room we all trooped back
to *Acrohc*. As there simply wasn't room, only one official came into
the cabin with me. Another officer stayed on deck and the rest
remained on the quay.

The man who came inside *Acrohc* was from the National Security
Police and was very proud of it. He checked the cabin thoroughly,
holding up things like a can of beans and packets of spices and
noodles to show the others on the quay what they were. They all
acknowledged his findings in chorus.

Inside the chart table he found strange things like my Nautical
Almanac, a folder full of papers, a book of radio signals, a log book.
They seemed puzzled by everything that was in English probably
only because they couldn't read it and he kept these things aside to
take back to the police station.

Then he checked the lockers and found more suspicious things like
the VHF hand-held radio, flares and a direction finder. 'This could
be terrorist material, we take that too.' Then we all walked to the
police station and on the way they explained that we were walking

because they didn't have the spare parts needed to fix their one and only police car.

At the station, they re-checked everything and they seemed reassured when they found a story of my trip so far written in French. They were still concerned that I had no visa, however, and said that they would have to telex the capital to get me one. I was rather surprised to hear they had a telex. I was told that I was to stay at the Motel Gina for the meantime, that I was not to leave there and that the owner would keep an eye on me. They also confiscated my radio, flares, and passport for the duration of my stay. They wanted to keep my camera too, but I protested loudly so they gave in.

I was relieved to be well received by the owner of the motel who was a Malgash lady with a French husband. They gave me a bungalow which although not luxurious was very clean and had a shower in it. While I stayed there I was constantly invited to dine with the owners which I did and was never charged for it.

The first evening they called in a doctor despite my protestations that I was alright. The doctor agreed with me. All the burns had healed except for a few infected areas. All I needed was a bit of a suntan on the new skin.

LOBSTER

The next day I received a visa for a week's duration and it didn't seem that there'd be any further problems. I was told that I could live aboard *Acrohc* but that I had to check in at Customs every time I went aboard. I was also told not to go wandering around at night and that I could only go as far as the city limits during the day.

I was quite upset by this treatment and even thought of leaving straight away but I didn't and was soon glad that I'd stayed. I'd been told what the rules were, but who said I had to stick to them! After I'd had a few beers with the police they let me do as I wished and Customs lost interest in me. I even went to a disco with some of the police and I enjoyed a picnic in the country with the motel owner and her family.

My favourite pastime though was dining at the motel. At every meal we talked about food specialties; it seemed to be the owner's way of finding out what I liked. And at each meal I would be presented with what I'd said I liked during the previous meal. The steak tartare was superb, as were her many ways of cooking lobster. My favourite dish was big rock oysters steamed with butter, garlic and parsley, but every meal was a treat.

I would breakfast on *Acrohc*, usually feasting on lobster. Every morning the local fishermen rowed by with their catch. And lobsters were cheap, so why not? I became quite friendly with the fishermen and one day they gave me a ride in a canoe which I nearly capsized. I can't understand how they bring in sharks of over two metres on them. We couldn't talk very easily but I did manage to understand from them that they were desperate for fishing gear. All I could give them though was a few hooks. I'd carry a lot more nylon line if I ever went back.

Many things were in short supply in Madagascar. Since the revolution times have been hard. Most of the French have gone and with them the few industries that they had developed. Even agriculture has been neglected. Almost everything is now imported and the exchange rate is such that it makes only the few tourists happy. But there is no doubt that they make good beer; it has even won an international prize.

The country itself is very beautiful—poor and wild like its inhabitants. Most people still live in small villages in primitive grass huts and I was surprised to see some coming into the town carrying spears called "Sagae". I was told they use them too! Murder, it

Fishermen of Madagascar
Huge sharks are caught from such dugout canoes

seemed, was not considered to be a major crime; being a terrorist or a South African was much worse.

The majority of the island's 10 million inhabitants are black and many live in the low country. In the higher regions live a people of either Malay or Chinese descent I'm not sure which, but one thing I am sure of is that the girls were most beautiful—amber skinned with Asiatic eyes and long, wavy black hair. That's not to say that I didn't like the other girls of Madagascar, or elsewhere!

All too soon my week came to an end. The burns had almost totally healed but now I seemed to be getting sciatic pain. Sciatica is the pinching of a spinal nerve caused by any number of things but usually a disc that's a little out of position. Whatever it is, it makes walking and even standing bloody painful. It wasn't new to me but I hadn't had it for quite a while. (I put it down to the cooler weather I was experiencing in the lower latitudes and sure enough, six months later when I returned to warmer climes it disappeared.) Now, however, it was horrible—the worst it had ever been. I could hardly walk for the pain. Some of the local hospital's staff were among the friends I'd made there and I was told by them that there was nothing that could be done about my condition on Madagascar. They also said that only lying down as much as possible would help. An operation for it would have meant returning to Reunion without *Acrohc*. I wouldn't have left her by herself even if the pain had really become unbearable.

I tried to get my visa extended so that I could rest for a few days but that caused problems. The president was soon to visit the town and I was still regarded as a possible terrorist. So I assured the police yet again that I was not going to South Africa and got my passport and belongings back. The day before I left, while I could still walk, I shopped for fruit and vegetables.

Just before I actually left a doctor brought me some tablets that were for the relief of sciatic pain. For a while I played with the idea of anchoring outside the harbour for a few days rest but then thought that I may as well be sailing.

Perhaps one day I'll return to Madagascar. I wonder if it will be the same or worse. The French had tried to 'civilise' the place, but I had visited it 20 short years after independence and it was noticeably regressing: buildings were falling into ruin, roads becoming unusable. Maybe, if I return, I'll find the few cars totally broken down and the post office (where even when I was there, stamps were stolen and letters thrown away instead of being forwarded) closed up and the people even poorer. Maybe it's just that they aren't ready for our kind of 'civilisation' yet!

I spent most of the next leg, the last stretch of the Indian Ocean, in bed. the log takes up the story.

June 12: All is well, Sciatica improving, lying down all the time. Just a couple of rain storms.

June 14: Stormy from noon. Still in bed.

June 16: Storm lasted till mid afternoon. Bad weather, haven't got out yet. Lost one more bucket in the night. That was only the second toilet bucket I'd lost and I was to lose a lot more by the end of the trip. I tied the bucket on the deck to make it easier to bring inside but in bad storms they were washed away.

June 17: Sunny at last. Two turtles came around at midday. Pain is now O.K.

June 19: Saw two leaping whales in the distance.

June 20: Got position check from cargo ship, only five miles different than mine on sextant.

One the eleventh day of that leg, *Acrohc* was overtaken by eight whales. At the time, I thought them to be orcas, but later found out they were sperm whales. I was climbing out of the cabin with a hot cup of coffee when I spotted them coming up behind. I was sailing slowly and *Acrohc* didn't seem to worry them. Only two were curious about us and one swam upside down very close to the keel to have a good look. In fact, they came so close that I got worried that they'd spray smelly water over the open hatch and into the cabin while I was taking pictures. Slowly the last one went past and I was left alone with a cold cup of coffee. It was my first encounter with whales.

June 22: Having second thoughts about this trip, maybe because no cigarettes, also cold weather and no wine left.

June 24: Strong winds in the night, worried about how close South African coast is.

June 25: Continuing strong following winds all day to gale force at night. Don't like this Mozambique Channel weather. My tactics

One of the great sperm whales I sighted on the trip

were to sail towards the coast during the day and at night sail parallel to it so that I could sleep knowing that I wouldn't run into it.

June 26: Heading west again with calmer winds. Saw a light at 1900 hours, must be Africa. Strange, no big excitement. Going south to sleep.

On June 27th, 17 days out of Madagascar, I neared the coast of Africa and headed toward a fishing launch that was anchored about one mile off shore. I went alongside and asked if they could spare me a cigarette. Unfortunately no-one smoked.

'You're flying an Australian flag, where are you from?' the skipper asked.

'Australia,' I replied. 'My last port of call was Madagascar. How far is Durban?'

He took a long look at *Acrohc* and then at my face to make sure, I assume, that I wasn't pulling his leg, 'Twenty miles . . . did you come all the way from Australia on "that" little boat?'

I assured him I had and then had to answer a hundred questions in five minutes. When I took my leave he was muttering, 'I should have brought my camera, they will never believe me.' I felt like a Martian or something!

I sailed south for Durban in a very light breeze.

Acrohc had sailed across the Indian Ocean and she was the smallest boat to have done so. It hadn't been easy though and I was glad it was over. I had actually broken a record already but I wasn't too excited. After all, it was only the one ocean—I was after the world record.

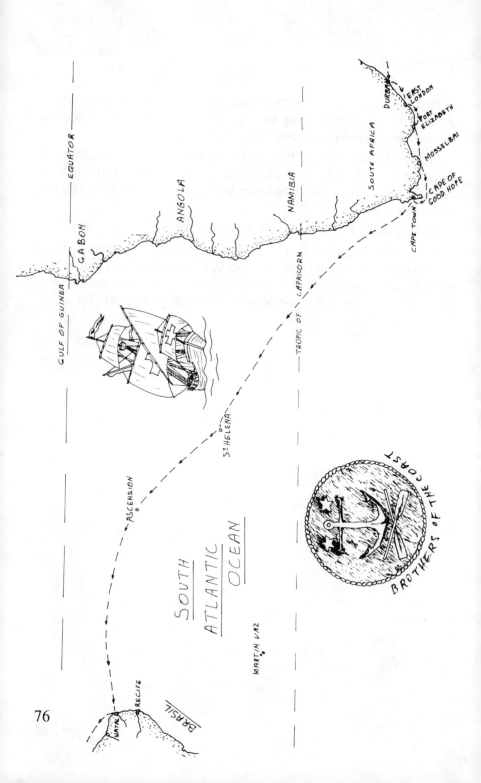

Chapter 6

CAPE OF STORMS

Next day, approaching Durban, I called up the Port Captain. He sent the police launch out to meet *Acrohc* outside the harbour when I was still a half a mile north of the breaker wall. Listening on the radio I could hear an argument going on between the captain of the launch and the Port Captain. The launch said, 'I'm outside the breaker wall and I can't see the yacht.'

'It's a 12 metre yacht flying an Australian flag and the sail has a yellow stripe,' came the reply.

After a while I interrupted with, 'It's 12 foot, not 12 metres.'

Finally they came alongside and gave me a tow. The skipper said, 'I don't believe it!' and repeated it all the way through the big harbour to the international jetty. We got there after dark and, judging by the number of people waiting for us, there must have been a lot of eavesdroppers on the VHF.

As soon as I was cleared I was taken to the yacht club. The beer was good but I felt a little confused among so many people all wanting to know everything about everything. All the noise seemed strange to me, the sciatica was still hurting and I was tired. I didn't know whether to excuse myself and go and have a shower, drink the next beer that was put in front of me, or just go to bed. I also had a lot of things on my mind like whether I could withdraw money with my credit card (not always possible in some countries). I also wanted to contact my family and start repairing the fire damage.

I was happy to have crossed the first ocean but it seemed as though I had become used to being alone. I felt uncomfortable in the crowd. I finally didn't have a shower, drank the next beer and, after a meal, I returned to *Acrohc* but only to find another group of yachties keen for a chat. There I started to relax; it was more peaceful and the open air felt good.

I went to bed late that night. It was cold, *Acrohc* was dirty and the burnt cabin ugly to look at and smelly, but I felt at home there. In fact, I usually refused the offer of a place to sleep, accepting only on rare occasions. *Acrohc* was small and didn't have many comforts but I was used to her, the bunk was comfortable and everything was within easy reach—it was my home.

The next day, while I was tied to the busy jetty, the questions kept pouring in. 'Where do you sleep, what do you eat, don't you feel lonely, aren't you afraid, where do you go to the bathroom? And my answers, 'I had a bucket but I lost it; lately I've been hanging over the side. No I don't hate people. Yes I built her myself.' And still more questions and answers. 'You must read a lot?' 'No, I've no room for books. No she's never capsized. Yes I can cook in there.' 'And what is that for? What do you do . . ?'

A man sitting on his launch about twenty metres away took pity on me and called across, 'Why don't you come and tie up to my boat.' I did and it was a good move not only because he had a good supply of cold beer, but he also offered me the run of his boat and the use of his dinghy to get ashore. Alan and I came to be good friends and *Acrohc* remained tied up to his boat most of the time I was there.

On my second day in Durban I had a nice surprise meeting up with two friends who I'd first met five years earlier in Brisbane when they were cruising around. I knew that they had been in Durban building a boat but I had thought that by the time I reached there they would have moved on. Bernard is Polish and Nadine is French. They had been building a 55 foot yacht, *Nanou,* in Durban and had been at it for about a year.

They came to see me as soon as they heard of my arrival. It was a great reunion and we chatted for hours, swapping sailing adventures. They had been all over the world in their old boat but having reached Durban, had decided it was time to sell her and build a new one. My arrival coincided with the launching of *Nanou.* Of course, she still had to be fitted out inside and I like working on boats so I couldn't resist helping my friends, besides, I needed a rest from sailing. In any event, December was supposed to be the best time of year to tackle the Cape of Good Hope and, that being the case, I had a few months to kill. We decided to try to finish *Nanou* by October so we could leave Durban together on my birthday.

The work on *Nanou* continued for the next three months, with me taking time off to repair the damage to *Acrohc's* interior. I recovered the cushions and relined almost all of the cabin and I replaced the cracked front porthole glass with plexiglass, which was the same material as the side portholes. She also got a free paint job, courtesy of a local chandler who added two boxing kangaroos to the bow as a nice finishing touch.

During her time ashore *Acrohc* had many visitors curious about her strange keel. I had to explain many times that I preferred the torpedo shaped ballast which kept the weight as low as possible and that the gap in the lower part of the keel was to reduce lateral resistance thus reducing the heel. The wings were not a copy of Australia II, the America's Cup winner—I was building *Acrohc* before they even revealed the famous winged keel—however, mine was designed that way for more or less the same reason, that is, to stop lateral drift. Being such a small boat, I knew that *Acrohc* would heel quite a lot, which would result in the keel no longer being vertical but rather at something like 30 to 40 degrees and it would then tend to slip sideways and rise. But with the wings, the boat's angle wouldn't matter; the keel would have some grip and the boat could only go one way: forward.

Further, because *Acrohc* was so short, she would have tended to horse a lot. The funny large plate on the bottom of the rudder was to stop horsing, which helped stabilise her and also made the rudder more efficient when she heeled a lot because the water could not escape through the bottom of the rudder. Of course, when all this extra wet surface was dirty with weeds and barnacles it contributed somewhat to slowing us, but this was more than compensated for by the more efficient sailing generally.

When I was building *Acrohc* I concentrated mainly on speed—the faster I could sail, the easier the entire trip would be—but I didn't neglect safety. The entire boat was welded together, each locker partition reinforcing the hull and acting as ribs. The keel was made of three ten millimetre aluminium plates that I laminated together for more flexibility so they wouldn't break. I built the rudder the same way. The boat was just about indestructible. People were often surprised to hear that *Acrohc* had no liferaft but I was and still am confident that with such a boat a liferaft was useless ... (yes, I know, the *Titanic* was also unsinkable).

After the fire damage had been repaired, *Acrohc* went on display in a shopping centre. I spent a week listening to remarks, some quite upsetting, like, 'They'll never let you out of the harbour you know,' and some pretty silly questions like, 'What do you do if there's a shark?' Actually that seemed to be the most popular question—as though sharks love to eat aluminium!

When all that was over, an 'official' relaunching of *Acrohc* was held. The Port Captain arrived with the Commodores of two yacht clubs, and representatives from both the local Australian and New Zealand Association plus the South African Navy and the Mayor of Durban. The latter was a nice guy and despite his advancing years did not hesitate to climb up the somewhat shaky ladder to look inside *Acrohc*. He also presented me with the key to the city.

I also received sponsorship in the shape of a new motor. It was an almost new 7.5 HP outboard, bigger than the old one which was only a year old but due to corrosion had aged prematurely and had become unreliable.

I spent some time sightseeing in the surrounds of Durban, always at the invitation of locals.

One outing was to see the Zulu villages in the Valley of the Thousand Hills. We went to a village especially arranged for tourists, but on the way we saw many real ones. I found those villages very interesting. Each was a collection of round grass huts, neatly arranged and surrounded by a high woven fence. At the 'tourist village' we were shown how the Zulus live, how they made their own beer and a large selection of their handicrafts. Apparently each village has its own witch doctor and witch doctor's apprentice who has to learn, amongst other things, how to read bones and mix potions . . . not all were medicinal either!

I was surprised to find that these particular Zulus had kept their culture, resisting the changing world around them. This is unlike

Serge poses with Zulu dancers

many other Zulus who have left their homes and travelled to the big cities. I'll never forget the night I stayed in a Zulu township.

Unlike the villages I had seen, it was ugly—the houses built of sticks, beaten earth and corrugated iron. I didn't see a single pane of glass except in the many abandoned cars that littered the place. There was no organisation whatsoever but the people seem content to live in these conditions, just waiting for the government to provide them with housing.

A few days after my visit to the black township, the racial fighting worsened and thereafter I was only able to visit white areas where invitations were frequent to 'braais' and I enjoyed long chats as we waited for the steaks to grill. South Africa is a complicated place.

There were a lot of good times on *Nanou*. Between jobs there was always time for a drink, usually with our many friends. Bernard, a good Pole, likes vodka as much as I do. This is probably why we are such good friends.

My sciatica was still bothering me but I was learning to live with it. A few trips to the chiropractor had relieved only the pressure on my wallet. What I really needed was sunshine; Durban was cold and windy at that time of year.

*****

The 5th of October, my birthday, arrived and work ceased on *Nanou;* we'd done it. She was a complete yacht with a crew of 11 and ready for the trip to Cape Town. It called for a party.

Acrohc was tied to *Nanou* and over a hundred people crowded the two boats. Most, of course, were on *Nanou* but *Acrohc* carried her fair share. Bernard decided that as a birthday present we should break the old record of nine people aboard *Acrohc*. We got fourteen volunteers, with Bernard and I standing on the spreaders holding onto the mast (actually, there was still room for a few more on the deck).

Five pages of my log book were filled with good wishes, names and addresses and a beautifully detailed drawing of *Acrohc* by one of my new friends, Gerry. He was a fanatic about wooden boats and I felt that he'd added the 'feeling' of wood to *Acrohc* in the drawing.

I had been well received in Durban. South Africans are quite involved in yachting so probably for that reason I was treated well. The media were also enthusiastic. Being on the front page is always flattering and in South Africa I made the front page about half a dozen times.

When the farewell celebrations were over *Acrohc* and *Nanou* were made ready to leave and we planned to meet up again in East London. That leg involved only 240 miles of coastal sailing, but anyone who knows the South African coast would take it very carefully. We had been in Durban long enough to get plenty of advice and to observe local weather patterns, which went like this: for about a week, the westerly wind blew in the opposite direction to the current off the coast. Then for two or three days the wind came from the northeast, going in the same direction as the current. This was when we had to make the move before it changed again and repeated the pattern, as the westerly wind blowing against the current created waves high enough to prevent even a cargo ship getting through. If I got caught in those conditions one option was to sail really close to the coastline to avoid the current and I wasn't keen on that because it meant that I'd have to keep a constant watch. The other option was to escape the current by sailing away from the coast but then I would encounter the easterly current further south and with unreasonable winds, I could be blown back to Mauritius. Either option was not the ideal. Good planning and a bit of luck were needed for this leg!

*****

Nanou and *Acrohc* were escorted out of the harbour by a lot of friends' boats. Outside the harbour a cruise boat came close to *Acrohc*, the people on board waved and took photos of her and although I thought I recognised some of the people I never did find out if it had been a special farewell cruise organised as a send off or if it was purely coincidental. In any event I waved back and quickly closed the hatch as it was blowing fairly hard. *Nanou* seemed to be sailing well on her 'shake down' cruise and I could imagine Bernard's excitement—sailing a new boat for the first time is always something to remember. Half an hour later though she was out of sight.

The weather was doing the right thing by us and there was plenty of wind but I had no intention of taking it easy and used my new outboard to go even faster. I wanted to reach East London before the wind changed. That year a fleet of thirty racing yachts had been caught by the westerly wind; only one finished the race. Some had been dismasted and one had disappeared completely. But I needn't have worried. With the strong following winds *Acrohc* didn't make less than three knots, despite the choppy seas and sometimes even with no sail at all. Still, it was rough and I couldn't help worrying about *Nanou*. Bernard and Nadine had a lot of experience at sea, but *Nanou* was a new yacht. *Acrohc* reached the harbour of East London at 8.00pm that night. In the dark we sailed through the rolling waves between the breaker walls and soon reached the calm waters of the river.

In the harbour a naval launch spotted me and showed me where I could tie up. There was no sign of *Nanou* and I became even more concerned about them.

I was relieved to have made the trip without being caught by the westerly winds but the rest of the voyage to Cape Town could be a different story.

A man called Otto met me at the jetty. He helped me tie *Acrohc* up alongside another yacht and then drove me to the yacht club where I was expected. It was a small club but what a welcome, the best reception so far! And I was the guest of honour at the ceremony for the start of the club's sailing season.

I stayed in East London for three days before leaving for Port Elizabeth, the next good port. There was still the risk of bad weather but the current wasn't as strong and contrary winds wouldn't create the gigantic waves I had been concerned about.

When I left, the same naval launch that had met me escorted me out of the harbour. It stayed with me for about a mile out in the rough seas then the crew waved and left me. But I was not quite alone; a lot of ships pass that way and I knew that I had to be extra careful. Somewhere in those waters *Supercilious*, a Venezuelan friend's yacht had collided with a cargo ship, despite having a crew of five to keep watch. They'd been lucky and only had minor damage. But with bad weather and poor visibility anything could happen. What were my chances? The sooner I reached the next harbour the better.

But this time the wind played up and I had to use the motor a lot. And when motoring straight into the wind the windvane was useless, so I had to stay at the helm battling against the choppy seas all the time. It was uncomfortable and tiring. In the middle of the first night I couldn't take any more of it and pointed away from the coast so that I could get some sleep. I didn't care where we ended up just as long as I could lie down and get some shut eye. Somehow we avoided being run over by a ship while I slept and the next morning I resumed the course for Port Elizabeth.

At first there was no wind, then there were headwinds—it seemed like we were getting nowhere. Later a thick fog came down and with the ensuing poor visibility we narrowly escaped colliding with a ship, which made me realise that the next one might not miss. But on the almost windless night I was still tired enough to neglect my half hourly watch system by oversleeping.

The next day the motor played up and it was only by repeatedly starting and restarting it that we made Port Elizabeth. Halfway into the harbour I was met by Olivier and Jacky, two of *Nanou's* crew, in her tender. I had been worried about them for nothing. The weather made them give East London a miss. I was pleased to see them again and the vodka wasn't spared.

And the journalists didn't spare me either. 'Why are you late?' they asked. 'If you could make it to East London in 52 hours why did it take more than three days for the same distance?' It had already been reported in the papers that I might have turned back because of bad weather. I was almost sorry to disappoint the journalists who now couldn't report that *Acrohc* had been run over, or that something had happened.

The Port Elizabeth yacht club wasn't as friendly as East London's but they let me use their crane and they helped me to lift *Acrohc* out of the water so that I could check her bottom. A paint company in Durban had sponsored me to the tune of a special antifouling coat which was supposed to last three years. It was something new and *Acrohc* was to be the guinea pig. The antifouling was still there and it would probably have lasted the three years, but the weeds and barnacles seemed to rather like it. A dirty hull could make us lose one or two knots; sometimes that was more than half her speed.

About a dozen people, mainly *Nanou's* crew, helped me scrub her bottom so it didn't take very long and I promised *Acrohc* a new coat of antifouling when we reached Cape Town. She seemed happy with that.

After three days, *Acrohc* and *Nanou* were ready to leave and we agreed to meet again at Knysna, the next port. Early that morning we found good winds from the south and *Nanou*, who was much faster, soon disappeared from sight. Although it was a bit rough the sailing was good right through the first day and night. The following morning there was no wind at all and I wouldn't have minded sleeping-in but then I realised that *Acrohc* had strange white portholes—fog on the menu! And it was really thick with visibility down to one hundred metres. I wasn't too worried, however, knowing that if there was anyone else out there, they'd be clinging to their radars. By late morning the fog had lifted but it was followed by rain, then head-winds, then calm.

These conditions continued until I neared Knysna so I decided not to stop. I would have liked to let *Nanou* know about my change of plans but they didn't have a radio. The entrance to the port is very tricky and I have never understood how Joshua Slocum managed to get in and out by sail alone; I had a motor and wasn't game to try it. It's amazing how soft we become; the more we make life comfortable, the softer we get. For example, I've been told that as recently as a hundred years ago in Italy people simply didn't have a calendar hanging on the wall to keep track of the days, but they could tell what day of the week, say, Christmas would be on by doing a few quick mental calculations referring to the phases of the moon. I would be lost without a calendar—and a digital one at that.

But getting back to the story, Joshua Slocum was the first man to circumnavigate the world solo. He did it in the 1890's on *Spray*, a 36 foot gaff-rigged yacht. I really admired him for although *Spray* was lot bigger than *Acrohc*, he achieved his ambition without any modern navigational aids like RDF or two way radios. An interesting comparison is that for the accurate time I could either refer to my digital watch or use the short wave radio. Joshua Slocum on the other hand had a mechanical clock . . . and he could only afford one that had a missing hand!

Anyway, I sailed on for Mossel Bay. I was getting sick and tired of that coast with its rough conditions and cold weather but I had no choice—it was far safer to head for the next harbour than take any unnecessary risks and besides it was only a couple of days away.

When I arrived at Mossel Bay, I radioed to find out where to tie up. I was told to tie onto two boats already at the jetty. It was 8.00pm and no-one was around. No reporters, no curious crowd, not even the owners of the two yachts nor the anonymous man who'd answered my radio call. I had to celebrate this so I went to a restaurant. From the restaurant I telephoned the yacht club at Knysna to try to find out the whereabouts of *Nanou* but no-one knew or had heard anything. I was worried that there were no good harbours before Cape Town, which was a long way off. However, the guy I spoke with did tell me that there was a Beerfest about to start there. I didn't want to miss that and, besides, I wanted to visit the place, which I had been told was beautiful. I decided to go back there by car and was lucky to get a lift with the Port Captain.

For two hours we drove through the beautiful countryside, eventually arriving at Knysna Valley where the trees grow very tall on the shores of a big lagoon. The entrance from the sea to the lagoon is a narrow opening, a sort of natural trench in a mountain, scattered with half submerged rocks which the waves broke over. I was glad that I hadn't tried to sail through that and I still can't understand how Slocum managed it.

I had fun at the Beerfest and the next morning got a lift back to Mossel Bay. I was eager to reach Cape Town and finish with this particularly nasty piece of coastline.

I bought more fuel and wished *Acrohc* good luck for the next leg. It would take us past Cape Agulhas which has a bad reputation and then on to the Cape of Good Hope (also called the Cape of Storms with good reason). The Cape of Good Hope is where the current from the Indian Ocean meets head on with the current coming the other way from the Atlantic. Add a good storm to that and it could mean trouble, not forgetting the danger of many ships.

SEAL

I left Mossel Bay on October 20 and met a friendly sea. It was good sailing all through that first day and night. It did rain, however, and the weather continued to get colder. Through the night I kept my usual watch system of one hour's sleep at a time.

On day two I discovered that my battery was flat as there hadn't been any sunshine to speak of for a good few weeks. So it was all lights out, including navigational. The wind had been increasing to gale force and the waves of up to five metres made sleep that night difficult. I was still a safe distance from Cape Agulhas but even knowing that didn't make sleeping any easier.

Next morning it was a bit calmer and I was able to run the motor to charge the battery. The waves were still big and the motor was often completely submerged but it kept going.

I was keeping about 15 miles away from the coast for safety, navigating by RDF or by sight when the coastline was visible. After a couple of hours of being reasonable, the wind picked up to gale force again. When it eased I sighted Cape Agulhas, (it was more a case of now you see it now you don't) and I knew then that I was only a day away from the Cape of Good Hope. That night the wind was good for sailing fast but not so good for sleeping and I was starting to get very tired.

The next day could be compared to a day in hell. We were south of the Cape of Good Hope and the waves were coming at us from every direction. The wind was blowing from the southwest but it had little effect on the waves which were simply doing their own thing. Somehow *Acrohc* was still managing to battle her way forward.

At exactly 5.00am, as the day broke, I sighted the dreaded Cape of Good Hope and the mountains rising behind it. It was a moment I'll always remember not so much for the sighting itself but more for how rough it was. And I'd already thought the weather was cold but now, coming into the Atlantic, it was colder still as the currents were coming direct from Antarctica.

I had planned to sail in the lee of the mountains hoping that they would break the force of the wind to some extent, but it was blowing stronger than ever. The waves had become more regular although they were still up to five metres high, or at least that's how high I estimated them to have been (it's always hard to judge the size of waves from a boat), but suddenly a barge-like ship passed within a few metres of *Acrohc* and when I recovered from the shock, I realised that the waves were much much higher than I estimated. *Acrohc* was going up and down with the waves but this ship was ploughing through them, its bow often going completely under water. The waves must have been closer to ten metres high!

I still had 40 miles to go before reaching Cape Town's Table Bay and the comforts of the harbour. The winds were right and we made good progress during the day but I was concerned about having to turn into headwinds once there to actually get into the bay. I was counting on the motor to help.

I finally reached the entrance to the bay just before dark and turned into the wind. After ten minutes of our making absolutely no progress, the motor stopped altogether, maybe as a result of spending so much time under water. The wind was now blowing at about 50 knots and to get into the bay I had to try to sail against it. I comforted myself with the thought that it would be sailable once inside the bay. However, in the meantime, there was nothing else to do but tack against the wind until something changed, and reduce sail as the wind blew stronger. But I had to reduce sail so much that I was only just holding my position. Then the wind reached 60 knots and was still getting stronger.

This was the fourth night with almost no sleep. I was feeling really tired and it was getting colder but at last I had reached the middle of the bay. We were still sailing one way for a couple of miles, turning before hitting rocks, and then sailing the other way. I wasn't getting any closer to the harbour but at least we weren't being blown out to sea.

Past midnight we were still doing the same thing. There were rocks on both sides of the bay so I had to stay awake. It would be another hour before I'd have to turn again, so I rested my head on a cushion and closed my eyes. I was careful not to fall asleep though and comforted myself with thoughts of a wind change.

By then the wind was about 70 knots and still increasing. *Acrohc* was heeling over at more than 45 degrees and I couldn't reduce sail any more or there would have been nothing left; she needed at least a little to keep moving forward.

I had been trying to keep a good lookout but all I could see were the distant city lights. Because of the spray I couldn't even see the shoreline. I wasn't going to get out of the cabin for a better look either; it was too cold. So far I'd managed to stay dry and I intended to stay that way.

After six hours of battle, the harbour was still over a mile away and I was still just managing to hold my position. But I certainly wasn't going to turn away now and end up who knew where and I wasn't going to call for help. A call for help would mean having to go on deck to secure a line for a tow and I'd get soaked and freezing which was out of the question! Already to keep warm in the cabin I kept the stove on with a pot upside down over the flame—it acted as a heater.

No, I wasn't going to call for help. I'd got myself into this situation of my own free will. How could I involve other people in my mess.

The wind had to change sometime. I'd just have to wait and soon it would be daylight and things would improve; at least I'd be able to see.

I tacked once more, sat back, covered myself with a blanket, rested my head on a cushion and closed my eyes. Often telling myself, 'Hey you, you're sleeping. Who is watching for the rocks?' And I'd reply, 'No, I'm not asleep. You see . . . I'm just resting my eyes. I'm so tired. See? I'm awake . . . '

At 4 o'clock there was a loud bang. It was the keel hitting the rocks. Then *Acrohc* dragged her keel over the rocks, turning sideways and through the porthole I saw the beach coming towards us. With a loud crash we hit the beach. The next wave slid us along it and as I opened the hatch, which was by then beside me, I felt one more wave pushing *Acrohc* higher up the beach.

The tide was on its way down and soon *Acrohc* lay on the beach out of reach of the waves. I didn't even bother going outside. I closed the hatch, pushed a cushion under my head and went back to sleep on the galley!

As I said before, what a hell of a day. And not apparently just for me but also for the city of Cape Town itself. In the summer months it is often hit by winds of up to 60 knots called the 'Southeaster'. This wind comes over the mountains that overlook the city, gaining force as it funnels its way through the valley. Just before it hits the city it roars over Table Mountain, so named for its several kilometre wide flat top. You can often see a layer of cloud sliding down Table Mountain, rather like a table cloth. These 'overflowing' white clouds often precede the Southeaster, but that day the Southeaster surpassed itself and was renamed the 'Black Southeaster'.

It blew at about 80 knots, the strongest wind the city had seen in years and it caused spectacular damage. Windows shattered, trees were uprooted, cars were overturned and many yachts broke their moorings. In one instance a wall was blown over onto fourteen cars. That day people flew without wings!

I wasn't the only one to have picked such nice weather for sailing. The fleet of maxi yachts taking part in the Whitbread Round the World Race had also been approaching Cape Town at the time and some weren't as lucky as I had been. One arrived without a mast and another had a bent mast; only a few survived intact.

Meanwhile back on Blouberg Beach where we had landed, I was freezing and still trying to get to sleep when a small boy came poking around, He didn't say much but he did ask me what was wrong. I remember giving him a sarcastic reply and then he disappeared. He must have called the police because they were next on the scene. Reporters followed, then the sea rescue arrived but it had gone past being a sea rescue job: because of the line of rocks by then exposed by the low tide it would have been impossible to attempt to drag *Acrohc* back into the water and besides, the wind was still blowing too hard. (It continued to blow that way for another week.)

I was driven to the yacht club, 20 kilometres away by road, to work out a plan of attack. They gave me coffee and sandwiches while someone went to call the crew of *Nanou*. This was a nice surprise. Because of bad weather at the last harbour they had headed straight for Cape Town. Bernard came . . . with the vodka just in case I was wounded.

By then the place was waking up and people were coming from everywhere to help. We decided that *Acrohc* should be brought to the club by road. Before I knew it I had a four-wheel drive, a trailer and a mobile crane at my disposal. Then about six car loads of people headed back for *Acrohc*. Half were volunteer helpers and half reporters.

We had to move fast before the tide came in again. First we had to move *Acrohc* higher up the beach, so we stripped her of her mast and anything else that would make her lighter. Then with people pushing, the four-wheel drive dragged her up the beach near the road so that the crane could lift her onto the trailer. The operation was a complete success and *Acrohc* was in the club's yard by that afternoon.

Grounding in Cape Town with Table Mountain in the background. Everyone helped.

The only mark from her beaching was a round dent, 15 centimetres wide, on her port side from when she first hit the beach. The keel, being an alloy tube full of lead, didn't show any big marks from hitting the rocks. So, all I had to do was put everything back together and do a spot of painting. Less than a week later she was back in the water with new antifouling, ready to go again.

Back in the water *Acrohc* was tied to *Nanou* and Bernard and I made plans to leave Cape Town after the Whitbread racers had left. This gave us just over a month to organise the next leg and see a bit of the Cape province.

The local yacht club was comfortable and had a friendly atmosphere and I would have been happy to spend my time there or on *Nanou* but I was 'kidnapped' by a journalist shortly after my arrival in Cape Town. Not that I complained about it because in her time off Melissa took me to all the places of interest. We had a walk on Table Mountain's famous flat top and had trips to the beautiful surrounding countryside where a lot of wine is made—good wine at that. We spent a lot of time together and contrary to what we'd first agreed, became quite attached. This book however, is not a love story, so on with the sailing.

All the famous Whitbread racers were in Cape Town at the time so the place was full of reporters from all over the world. When they saw *Acrohc*, of course, they wanted a story.

One day I was approached by a journalist from a French magazine. I gave him a complicated piece of advice as to what he could do with his notebook as I thought he was from a magazine that had rejected an article I'd sent them. But he insisted that they'd never received anything. I checked my records and sure enough I had sent the article in question to their opposition. I was a bit embarrassed but he was understanding and we reached an agreement for them to publish the stories that I would send them from then on.

So now I was selling my stories to both a French and an Australian magazine. While I was in Cape Town I managed to sell a short article to a local magazine. It wasn't much but I was doing better than when I'd first set out.

I met a lot of people from the local yachting community and also the crews of the Whitbread racers who were interesting to talk to. I was impressed by the size of the boats but I did feel that they weren't as strong as they could have been.

I also met Joshua Taylor, a 76 year old who was sailing the world on his yacht *Comitan* and mostly by himself. We still keep in touch and I am proud to have met him. I hope that when I reach 70 I'll be like him—still able to sail around.

Glory was another boat that was in Cape Town while I was there. She was owned by Sir Henry Pigott and I had seen her when I was in Darwin. She was a small yacht, just under 20 foot, with an inboard motor and very roomy for her size. She was junk-rigged but I didn't know that at the time as she was in dry storage for the cyclone season and had her mast removed. I didn't meet Sir Henry then as he was in England catching up with his family.

One morning at the club, I was told that someone was looking for me. It turned out to be Sir Henry who had finally caught up with me. I learned from him that he was also setting a record, the smallest boat to 'solo' circumnavigate the world. I was only after the record for the smallest boat to do so but I would actually break his record at the same time, although not by choice. I felt bad about it but he wasn't too worried as he would complete his circumnavigation in a few months from then and, as I had over a year of sailing still to do, the record would be his for some time.

As with Joshua, Henry and I had the same kind of stories to tell each other. We lived in the same sort of world. There was us and there were the 'others'. I had felt the same way in Darwin when I'd met Gerard and Philippe. Gerard had sailed an inflatable raft, equipped with sails and motors from Sydney to Darwin. He had spent a lot of

Joshua Taylor, 76, on Comitan leaving St Helena

Sir Henry Pigott's 20 foot yacht, Glory, also after the record to SOLO circumnavigate in the smallest boat. He kept the record for one year.

money preparing the raft and had hoped to be able to make a video of the Australian coast to finance an around-Australia trip. But in Darwin, for reasons best known only to himself, he gave up. Adventure seeking though, was part of him and by the time I left Darwin he was already planning another trip along the same lines.

Philippe, when I met him in Darwin, was married and simply cruising around on a yacht. However, in his younger days he and a friend had sailed from Indonesia to Darwin in a dugout canoe! (The idea of making a long trip on an outrigger appeals to me too. Maybe one day I'll look into it . . .).

Another yacht I met in Cape Town was *Mallamoc* which was crewed by a couple, François and Anne-Marie, and their two year old daughter, Silvie. Silvie couldn't pronounce *Acrohc* so she called her Little Mallamoc. François and Anne-Marie were originally from

France and they had been working in Noumea and compiling news for the French ORTF (Organisation de Radio et Television Française). They had been transferred from Noumea to French Guiana and were on their way there. They were only in Cape Town for a few days but when I reached French Guiana I got to know the family better. Sylvie, I was told, didn't mind sailing and in fact she even gave a hand!

*****

The Whitbread Race was on again and I took *Acrohc* out in the bay to see the big yachts off.

Nanou and I were about ready to go too. Final arrangement had to be made like me sorting out the charts. I had so many charts wedged into the chart table that it was getting too heavy to slide in or out so I sent the old ones home, together with some accumulated junk.

I had given all the extra food I had left over from stocking up at Darwin to the poor people of Mauritius, Madagascar and Durban— 200 tins, flour, cereals and milk powder. I couldn't keep this food anyway as it was already a year old and I couldn't risk getting food poisoning at sea. So I left South Africa with only fresh supplies. This time I had a better idea of what I would need so I was more moderate in the supermarket. I bought a lot of vegetables and fruit but still had a little spare room for a few duty free bottles!

We were ready to go. *Nanou* was going to take a different route. They were heading towards Rio for the carnival, then would sail up the Brazilian coast and hopefully we'd meet up again. I was to follow the current and the tradewinds to north Brazil, going via St. Helena Island.

It was December 1985, 18 months since I'd started my voyage. If the winds were as predicted I'd be at St. Helena just after Christmas. Only one thousand eight hundred miles before I'd see someone again!

The J. family. Walker.
40 Mrs. J Cornelius
P.O. Box 30328
Les Marais
0038

THATS ONE
BIG CANOE, I
ALWAYS WAS IMPRESSED THAT IT
COULD CARRY 8 PEOPLE
FAIR WINDS SERGIO

Jerry WALKER.

6/29/85

Chapter 7

THE ATLANTIC

In a way I was glad to be leaving that cold and windy city and I was also looking forward to seeing a new and different place. But I was sorry too. I'd had a good time in South Africa and had been treated well by the South Africans. White or black they were all nice

Nanou leaving Cape Town

people and I think it's such a shame that the country suffers from so much racial tension. I hope one day they'll find a solution.

It was early in the morning, the wind was good and we had been cleared to leave the country. *Nanou* and *Acrohc* sailed out of the harbour together but I was soon left behind. One drawback of cruising is that you make good friends in the various ports but the chances of ever meeting them again are slim.

At first there were a lot of ships in the area but after a few days I was completely alone with the strong following wind making *Acrohc* roll violently in the cold choppy sea.

The sailing was uncomfortable but we were making three knots and doing nicely until a large wave came from nowhere and knocked *Acrohc* over, almost capsizing her. Because of the cold I had everything closed up, but I hadn't locked the hatch properly and it opened, letting a lot of water in the cabin. Lots of things got wet including my electric clock, which never recovered. The new echosounder I'd bought in Cape Town also got water in it, but I later dismantled it and sprayed it with penetrating oil. It continued to work fairly well. The wet blankets and cushions had to wait for some sunshine.

The eighth day out I ran out of cigarettes and this time I swore that I would give up for good. Ha! Every time I reached a port I took it up again. The following day the sun actually came out and I tried to get a sextant fix. It had been six months since I'd used the sextant and it took me a few days to learn how to use it again.

I felt very alone on that leg and often found myself looking around for something to busy myself with. I was missing the visits of dolphins and birds and even the pilot fish that briefly escorted me on the fourteenth day abandoned me; why was the South Atlantic so deserted? I remembered seeing lots of flying fish when I'd sailed those same waters as a passenger on a liner to Australia 14 years earlier. There was never a dull moment then . . . and I had all the luxuries as well!

It was Christmas Day when *Acrohc* crossed the Greenwich meridian. So I celebrated Christmas on the same day as the English by having a few drinks and a chocolate pudding with chocolate-rum sauce. But something was wrong. This trip just didn't seem like the others. I'd had rougher weather on the earlier legs so it couldn't be that. I didn't want to be alone anymore. I wanted to see my family and enjoy a few comforts. I started to feel like giving up this 'round the world stuff. I was sick of sailing in a boat so small that I couldn't even get up and take a walk or have a shower when I felt like it.

But the more I thought of giving up the angrier I got. I couldn't throw away all I'd done so far. Everyone was following my progress and, even if I didn't care about what people would say, how could I ever respect myself or have the courage to start any other projects if I didn't go through with this one. I just had to keep going. After all, I was half way home and the hardest part was behind me.

I don't know what really brought on this attitude, but I suspect that I'd been too comfortable in Cape Town. I'd made a lot of friends and, after living in a flat for a month, life on *Acrohc* was difficult. Perhaps it was love? No, that was impossible. I'd come too far and seen too much to have fallen for a girl that I'd only known a month . . . maybe that was the trouble? But I knew that whatever 'disease' it was I had to get over it and go on.

We encountered all sorts of nasty Atlantic weather but at least we had favourable winds. On New Year's Eve we were close to St. Helena and I wrote everything that happened that day in the log (just, I think, to keep busy). I may as well include it as it will give you an idea of a fairly typical day. Feel free to skip it if it bores you. I'll understand.

December 31st, 1985: Slept badly because land is close, woke up often to check. 4.30am got faint RDF signal from St. Helena. Had muesli breakfast in bed and back to sleep. 8.30, coffee, sunny day so I sat outside eating biscuits. 9.30, tea, then converted the bunk into a sitting position and slept on to 11.00am. All day often looking for land, expected time of arrival: night. From 11.00 to before noon, drank water, snacks, rum, coffee. 12.20, finished sextant noon position, 17° South, 4°45' West, still 65 miles to go. ETA, early morning, RDF nil at 12.45. Brush my teeth, sun canopy up, finger in the chocolate spread, rum. 3.30, tea, the BBC still playing sometimes clearly, biscuits. 5.00pm was cleaning binoculars and started to rain, canopy in, reduced sail. News programme on radio, changed station. False alarm, no rain. 5.15, Rum. 5.40, getting colder, closed the hatch, rum, BBC back on lots of news, getting dark, time to cook. 8.00, finished eating noodles with onion and tomato sauce, coffee, rum, toilet outside. 8.20 still not sighted St. Helena lights. 8.30, make the bed, tired, will take naps and watch out for land in case sextant bearing was wrong, keep depth sounder on with alarm at 30 metres. 12.30am, New Year slept too good, no lights so back to bed after checking depth sounder, woke up at 1.30am, no land. 2.30, no land, using kitchen timer for alarm clock. 3.30, no land. 4.30, no land. 5.30 no more beeps on RDF and still no local broadcast, slow going at night but should see it now. Daylight, muesli, coffee. 6.30am, toilet, sun is out, snooze to 7.30, very tired and sleepy, still no land, snacks, rain hiding the sun, nearly no wind, boat speed one knot first time since Cape Town, tried running the motor, no good, started raining half way through spark plug cleaning. 8.00am, clipped beard, tried motor again, no good, rain again. 8.45, motor still won't go, then saw land about ten miles, not bad for sextant work, a bit happy, rum. Radio St. Helena finally. 11.30, tried many times to start the motor and gave up, had two apples and coffee, shampoo then swim, still going slow. Half sun at noon, reached island at 12.00pm. Keeping awake to sail around to Jamestown, almost no wind behind the island, very close to rocks but calm sea, no motor so paddled some of the way with spinnaker pole. 5.07 anchored next to Glory in 20 metres of water, tired.

There you have it. Of course, I didn't always drink so much but it was New Year and I was approaching a new port.

Henry Pigott had left the Cape after me, but *Glory* was much faster and they'd arrived before me. Actually, most yachts make that passage in two to three weeks so I couldn't complain about *Acrohc's* time of 21 days.

The following morning I learned that *Nanou* had made a detour to St. Helena but had left the day before I'd arrived. It was a shame but I was comforted by the bottle of vodka Bernard had left behind.

During that first week on St. Helena, Josh arrived. He had been sailing alone as he couldn't find a crew in Cape Town. Not that he really needed one. He was 76 but he was more capable than many of the sailors I'd met. He invited me on board for a drink as soon as he arrived, but I suggested that he might need a rest first. But, he argued strongly, 'Who's tired? The self-steering did all the work. It was boring. I read ten books on the trip.' (Maybe that was why, two weeks later when he left St. Helena, he had a crewmember—a nice 30 year old brunette—and fewer books.)

The following week, John Snowdon dropped by on his 25 foot yacht, *Tarmin*. Originally from America, he was on his third circumnavigation and when I met him I recalled Sir Henry's remark, 'There are a lot more nuts afloat than you think.'

They are all members of the Slocum Society and influenced me to join. The Society keeps its members informed of everyone's whereabouts via monthly newsletters which is a good way for cruising yachts to keep in touch. I don't regret joining and I've been made a life member for completing a circumnavigation.

I had planned to stay for one week on St. Helena but ended up staying six. I'd been told that there was a bank so I would be able to withdraw money. The island is British so I wasn't expecting any problems, thinking that even if my credit cards weren't accepted I could at least get a telex transfer from home. But as it turned out the bank didn't know anything about credit cards and the telex fund transfer from my family got lost. If I'd have known I would have left the island straight away as I had enough supplies to reach Brazil. As it was, each day I waited there I got into more debt, mostly from telephone calls home.

Napoleon had said, 'The English sent me to die on this rock.' I knew how he felt. But I wasn't in trouble nor in danger of starving because Ann Sim, the owner of a restaurant, was a very nice lady who gave me credit (and besides, there was plenty of food on *Acrohc*). Almost every day I walked to the restaurant to ask if there was any news of my telex and every day Ann would answer, 'Nothing today, love. Do you need cigarettes? Do you need money? Here take five pounds. Tomorrow's Saturday and there's a dance in town. You should go and have fun. Have you eaten? . . . '

I spent the days walking around the island which is small but beautiful. It is mostly volcanic rock but very lush and green in the centre, especially where Napoleon's house was situated. However, he didn't like it on St. Helena even though he had many of his generals and members of his family for company. Some say he was poisoned by his staff (who hoped that they'd be sent home) but it was never proven. I believe his stomach ulcer killed him and I felt a bit like him! I was stranded there and my ulcer was starting to play up because of it too.

Usually my ulcer only hurt when I didn't have a boat, but the missing telex was really getting on my nerves. Apparently it turned up on some other St. Helena Island (there are at least five others) but a few weeks later I gave up on it. I telephoned my brother Henry and asked him to send a cheque by mail to Melissa in Cape Town; she could then forward it to me on the island's monthly supply ship. If all went well, I should have the money in two weeks.

In the meantime I kept busy any way I could. Dozens of yachts called in at St. Helena on their way to the Americas or Europe and many I'd met in South Africa called in. I was considered to be a good jack of all trades so I often helped with repairs on the various boats. It was amazing how many yachts had something broken. I often thought of opening a boat repair shop once I got back home. (My brothers had closed the boat building yard only two months after I'd left. They hadn't liked that kind of work and I couldn't blame them; after all, I'd left it myself!)

The inhabitants of St. Helena are the descendants of slaves from many races. The island had been a popular port of call for the slave traders en route from Africa. Many of them escaped there and made the island their home. I was told that the locals had often helped escapees and had continued to do so until slavery was finally abolished everywhere.

Now they all live well and, because it's such a close community, there is no poverty at all on the island. I found the locals to be nice if a bit shy. But this shyness or modesty is probably because of their isolation. It is certainly an island I want to visit again.

One Friday as I came back from a fishing trip with one of the locals, I saw Anne waving from the jetty, or I should say steps. (There is no jetty on the island because of the constant rollers. To get ashore we had to grab a rope hanging from above the steps and hold on to it as we jumped from the dinghy onto the steps; then haul the dinghy up. When it was rough there was, quite simply, no going ashore! In fact the supplies for the island come only by ship. They are ferried from the ship, which anchors off shore, by barges and a crane is used to winch the goods out.) Anyway, Ann was waiting on the steps for us yelling, 'The money's arrived!'

I wasn't expecting it as the supply ship hadn't arrived, however it turned out that it had been sent to South Africa by mail and telexed from there. This telex didn't get lost but even now I'd still like to know what happened to the first one—maybe it was sent to Saint Helena herself in Paradise!

Two days later I had paid all my debts and the port dues, got back my passport, which there as in many places had been held by Immigration for the duration of my stay, and was ready to leave. The end of the sailing season was very close and it was time for *Acrohc* to take one more step towards home.

This time I had no trouble adjusting to life at sea again. The anchorage at St. Helena had been a bit rough so it was much the same out at sea. I'd been thinking of making a detour to Miami but the six week delay at St. Helena put an end to that. It was late in the sailing season and I knew there would be cyclones in the Caribbean Sea. I was sick of bad weather. I wanted to get home by the shortest and easiest route, via Ascension Island.

There were 700 miles to go to Ascension. The weather was good, there were birds around, the pilot fish came back to escort us and the dolphins came to visit again.

On the second day I decided the time had come to catch a fish! And by then I had all the gear as a Durban lure manufacturer had provided me with a strong line, mounted with a shock rubber and a large assortment of lures and hooks. This time there would be no excuse for failure.

A dorado soon took the bait and to my surprise nothing broke and I was able to pull it on deck. It was over a metre long and I was sorry

Drying out the catch, in the Atlantic

that I didn't have a wide angle lens for my camera. There was enough meat to keep me going for a few days.

The other dorados kept swimming around *Acrohc*, maybe looking for the missing one, and I couldn't resist getting another one with my spear gun. It was a shame to kill such beautiful fish, but I needed the fresh food and sadly that is what survival is all about. These fish change colours and the two I caught turned from yellow to blue, golden and silver. None of the meat was wasted. I ate a lot of fresh meat but mainly I filleted and hung it up to dry in the rigging or preserved it in jars.

We continued along with running winds. Some days were better than others but overall I couldn't complain. In fact, one day we covered just over a hundred miles which was close to a record; according to my sextant, the best day's run had been 120 miles.

One day before sun up, something started pulling on the trawling line. It was a tuna, which was shorter but much fatter and stronger than a dorado. Three hours later I finally had it tied by the tail to a rope trailing behind *Acrohc*, ready for filleting. But first I had to recover from the backache it gave me in the fight it put up. There was a lot more meat on it than either of the dorados but I still didn't waste any of it and in a few days it was all gone. I liked to nibble on the bits of dried meat and without really realising it, I got through most of it.

Eleven days had passed when I sighted Ascension Island. As usual, I had started looking out for land too soon and lost a lot of sleep unnecessarily. But I couldn't trust my sextant readings. It was easy to make a ten mile error, especially with the boat moving so much and being able to see the horizon only when lifted up by a wave.

By nightfall we were sailing around the island. I contacted the authorities and finally anchored where I was told to in the darkness. The authorities on Ascension usually only allow yachts to stay there for two days, but this is enough time to have a look around. It is a small island with no permanent inhabitants, but both the British and the Americans have military bases there. The terrain is all volcanic like St. Helena but there was only a little vegetation in the centre of the island. The rest of it was made up of the craters of extinct volcanoes.

There are, however, hundreds of aerials of every shape and size imaginable. The island is used for communications relays because of its mid South Atlantic location. And for me it was the midpoint of the trip. I had sailed half way around the world in two years. Mind you, I had spent six months cruising the Barrier Reef and six months in South Africa so I estimated that if all went well I'd be home in one more year. It seemed a long time but I knew it would be 'down hill all the way'—except for one stretch after Panama.

The charts showed favourable winds all the way home and there were lots of nice places to see on the way. I had been told that the Marquesas were enchanting and I'd been wanting to visit Tonga for a long time. And there was Tahiti! I made plans to have a bit of rest in Brazil, perhaps visiting the Amazon jungle. Thinking of the trip this way made it seem shorter . . . I'd be in Brazil in a few weeks and then there'd be only one more ocean left to cross.

My only regret on leaving Ascension was that I hadn't spent a night on the beach to see the sea turtles laying their eggs in the sand. I have no valid excuse as, although the steps to get ashore were worse than the ones at St. Helena, I could have got a lift in with the crew of a tanker which was in the same anchorage as *Acrohc*, in their tender. But I just didn't feel like it. Maybe I just wanted to catch up on a bit of sleep.

The winds were good and so was the current. I was looking forward to the cold beer I'd have when I reached Natal, only 1,200 miles away.

By evening Ascension Island was already out of sight and in its place was a long and beautiful rainbow.

A few days later found us in a sloppy sea with wind from the stern, not helping to stabilise *Acrohc*. It was difficult to do anything in those conditions and sleeping was soon a problem—I could only last a few days without proper sleep before I'd start hearing things.

Four days later nothing had changed except that evening it rained cats and dogs. But the rain only lasted for ten minutes and when it stopped the wind died. This confused the waves which started going every which way, colliding into each other with great two metre splashes. *Acrohc* was stuck in the middle of the mess and with no wind to stabilise her, we were tossed around badly. A short time later the wind came back but from a different direction and the waves got even crazier. We must have been in the crossroads of two currents. By dinner time things had settled down and I cooked myself a simple meal. Then I saw a ship ahead of us and as I couldn't work out which way they were going, I tried to contact them. They didn't reply though and when they were a bit closer, I saw that it was a Japanese long-line fishing boat.

On the seventh day I was rudely awakened by a sort of rubbing noise coming from the deck. A four foot tuna was hooked on the trawling line. This time, more experienced, I had little trouble bringing it on board. After breakfast I set to work on it, laying it over the winches in front of the cabin and tying both ends of it to the rigging to stop it falling back into the water. The last tuna had been tasty and had kept well so I cut this one up the same way. A couple of hours later I had cut all the flesh into long strips and put them in a large bowl ready to be rolled in a mixture of vinegar, salt and spices before I would tie each strip onto a line that I'd attach to the rigging. I would bring the drying meat in at night and put it out again in the mornings. That way, in three days, I would have plenty of dried meat to nibble on.

I'd hung about a third of the meat up on the rigging when I reached for the bowl for another strip and couldn't find it. It had fallen over the side! I couldn't leave all that meat behind after all the work I'd done preparing it and besides, that was my only bowl. If I was fast enough I should be able to turn around and with a bit of luck find the bowl.

Within seconds I had furled the sail and lowered the outboard. I had done all this before when a breakfast bowl had gone overboard

111

so I knew what I was doing. But this time the outboard didn't cooperate and I even imagined it saying, 'My throttle cable is stuck.'

'I oiled you last week,' I said aloud to it (plus some other words).

'Well, I'm not going to start so you may as well forget about the fish.'

I tried a few threats. 'What if I undo those two bolts so you fall in the water! After all, I'm carrying your weight all around the world and when I need you, you don't start.'

But it still refused to start and I forgot about the fish as by that time we were too far away from where it might have been and, by sailing against the wind, we'd never find it. I did seriously think about dropping the motor over the side though, but didn't in the end—it was only a stuck cable.

The rest of the day passed uneventfully except I saw a whale going along peacefully in the opposite direction to me.

The afternoon of the next day there was no wind but I didn't mind as it meant I could relax and cook a decent meal. That night I saw a strong light and hoped that it was coming from a ship (if it wasn't I was in the wrong place). But there was no mistake that it was from a ship—probably one of the Japanese boats looking for its lines. Their way of fishing is to put a lot of hooks on a strong line with an anchor at one end and a red buoy on the other. They toss the lot overboard and come back later to pick it up. One day I saw three of the red buoys, nearly running into one . . . you'd think that the sea would be too big a place to run into something like a buoy.

The short wave radio was a good way to pass the time in the evenings. One night I listened to a programme about Halley's Comet which was apparently going to meet with the satellite Giotto. The announcer said that the satellite was travelling at fifty times the speed of a bullet. *Acrohc* was doing two knots at the time and I'd have been happy to do just the speed of a bullet, not fifty times the speed. I felt a bit disgusted. But, sometime later they lost contact with the satellite; apparently it had been knocked out by something and I felt a bit better—*Acrohc* might be slow but she was still going. Of course, we could also be 'knocked out' by one of those fishing boats . . .

By now the weather was warmer, just the way I liked it.

A short rain storm gave me the chance to shampoo my hair and although the weather stayed overcast for a few days, sailing conditions were good. My new occupation at night was chasing birds away who were trying to nestle on the top of the hatch. I wouldn't have minded except they squabbled and fought over the same spot just when I was trying to sleep and as this took place just above my head, I wasn't about to put up with it. And when they weren't fighting I still knew they were there by the white 'stuff' dribbling down the porthole. I didn't like the look of it and I certainly didn't like the smell. The best way to get rid of them was to push them into the water with a pole just as they were coming in to land on the boat. Usually after a couple of dunkings they'd give up.

On the eleventh day the weather was still good and we crossed the halfway mark; only 600 miles to go. I estimated that if the weather held I'd be drinking a cold beer in about a week. In the meantime I cooked the last of the fresh vegetables I'd been able to get on Ascension Island. From then on it was dehydrated and tinned food.

The bread had only lasted seven days even though I had dried it in the sun and sprinkled it with vinegar to stop it going mouldy. But this wasn't a problem because I could always make pancakes or eat dry biscuits instead. Eggs weren't a problem, they always lasted well. What I couldn't 'keep' was wine; it just kept disappearing!

That evening the air was fresh and *Acrohc's* rocking was gentle and peaceful. The new moon looked good among the millions of brilliant stars and I didn't have a care in the world. I was now starting to enjoy the sailing.

Of course, all good things come to an end. By nightfall the wind was gusty and *Acrohc* was rolling like hell so I couldn't sleep. The next morning I had to clear the deck of half a dozen dead and smelly flying fish before breakfast which I just managed to eat without spilling everywhere. The day was overcast with threatening showers. It was too hot to keep the hatch closed but too windy to put the sun shade up and as a result I got sunburned despite the clouds. And the rolling was getting to me, not to mention trying to cook dinner.

All of this would be enough to make anyone in his right mind give up the whole thing for a seat in a comfortable air-conditioned bar with a blonde on his lap. But I couldn't and wouldn't give it up. The more I sailed, the less I could even think of giving up so I just had to put up with it.

That night a beauty of a storm hit us. It hung around until morning and it took all of that next day for the wind and seas to calm down. By dusk, the sky looked just as threatening as it did the previous night, as though it was ready to start the whole thing over again. This time I went for the bottle of gin but the storm didn't come and the next day we were becalmed.

Evening again and this time we had a clear sky and a southerly wind which I hoped would last for the remaining 250 miles . . . of course, it didn't.

I got to understanding why Columbus' men wanted to throw him overboard when they sailed in those waters, especially if they'd had the same weather and were sailing at a maximum speed of half a knot with the sails continually flapping and sauna-like humidity. There were no fish and rarely even a seabird. When a squall blew up the wind would turn around completely, blowing at thirty knots or more for about 30 seconds or so.

I would have hated to have that kind of weather sailing in a square rigger with its large sails. But thanks to Columbus, I at least knew what was ahead of me. I could also listen to Radio Brazil and I had no upset crew to throw me over the side.

One thing I did envy him was his helmsman. With the light wind, my self-steering wasn't working efficiently and we were constantly off course. I had to keep a close eye on the compass and at least every five minutes I had to put *Acrohc* back on course. We were going so slowly that I didn't want to waste any headway. Often for a break I would go for a swim, but always keeping a sharp look out for one of the squalls which, luckily, I could see coming while they were still at some distance—either by seeing the quickly approaching black clouds or by the sound of the heavy downpour. While I was in the water I never missed a chance to clean the hull.

That evening I met *Ravens-Cray*, an English ship on its way to Rio. It was good to have a conversation with a human being, even if it was on VHF. They gave me a position fix which differed by 60 miles from mine. I panicked for a while, but reworking my calculations I discovered my error—the sun was now passing north of the Equator and that made the system of working a bit different.

During the night I got up quickly when I heard engine noises. It was a ship heading north that passed only 100 metres ahead of *Acrohc*. I wasn't running lights as the battery couldn't keep a light running every night. To do this I would have needed a bigger solar panel of at least three amps; I only had a 30cm by 30cm panel which just gave half an amp. Maybe it was silly to try to save a few hundred dollars by choosing the smaller panel but I knew that most cargo ships don't keep a watch on the open sea anyway; their routes are traced by a central computer so they don't run into each other—it's just too bad if you're in a yacht and happen to get in the way. I was obviously in a shipping lane so I just had to keep alert. I didn't mind getting up that night as the sky was clear and I saw Halley's Comet for the only time; for the rest of the trip it was obscured by clouds.

At daybreak another ship passed me. I was nearing the coast and would have to be extra careful.

Dorados were swimming around *Acrohc* but we were going so slowly that they ignored the lure trailing behind. I picked up the line and splashed it on the water. The fish got a bit excited and presto, fresh fish for breakfast. This came just in time as the last tuna had gone mouldy because there hadn't been enough sun to dry it properly.

The time passed as slowly as we were sailing. We'd been at it for 18 days, covering only 20 miles a day for the last four days. The current just wasn't helping and I still had 100 miles to go; it really felt like I was getting nowhere . . . slowly!

As night fell one more ship passed, reminding me to be alert. There was almost no wind at all and if a ship came my way I'd have to start the motor to get out of its path. That night I slept with one eye open until I heard engine noises. I knew just what to do. Step 1—don't bother to really wake up. Step 2—try to find out where the noise is coming from. Then, if it was coming straight for us and was too close to do anything about, go straight on to Step 4 (get back in, lock the hatch, brace yourself and learn to pray). But if it was still some distance away, there was Step 3 which meant lowering the motor, hoping it would start and if so, moving quickly out of the way.

So here was my chance to put my plans into action. I jumped up and looked around for the source of the noise. Ships are usually easy to see at night, especially at close range, as they keep a lot of lights running. But I couldn't see a ship. I woke up a bit more and still couldn't see one. I could hear the sound of a big engine clearly but there was nothing to see.

Ten minutes later I was still standing up looking around and feeling pretty stupid. Then I finally realised that the engine noise was not from a boat at all but from a large plane passing overhead!

It was still calm and I was nearing land so I had to try and get as much sleep as possible while it was still relatively safe. But some time later I jumped out of bed again as I could hear something else close by. It was only dolphins splashing around but even though I knew I should try to get back to sleep, I stayed out watching them in the darkened sea. I was always intrigued by the way they played with *Acrohc* as though she were a toy. Often they would try to make her race them, but when she didn't respond (she was usually going too slowly for them) they'd lose interest. But that night they were in luck. The wind suddenly came up and *Acrohc* started sailing at her best speed in the waveless sea. In their excitement they raced ahead of us, leaping high out of the water as I'd never seen before. It was as though they thought that *Acrohc* had woken up to play with them. Maybe she had. I watched them for a while and then tried to get some sleep before the sun came up.

We sailed well the next day and by evening a white light was visible which I could tell wasn't the light of a ship. According to my calculations it was land. But this light was climbing upwards into the sky and disappearing, not like usual lighthouse lights which sweep sideways before disappearing. Five minutes later the light reappeared and did the same thing again. I'd never seen a lighthouse light like that before and spent hours wondering what kind of new light the Brazilians had invented and whether it meant anything to ships. As I got closer, it started making sense. There was an airport near the coast and the lights belonged to aeroplanes which were taking off and then banking. Simple wasn't it!?!

Later I saw the light I'd really been looking for, the light from the lighthouse near Natal. All I had to do was sail towards it and I'd enter the river.

We'd crossed another ocean in 52 days of sailing time. Not so bad after all.

Chapter 8

MUD!

By three o'clock in the morning we had reached the Natal "Yate Clube". I asked the night watchman where I could anchor *Acrohc* and he told me it was okay to tie her to the front of the jetty. You may be wondering how I communicated with the fellow in his own Portuguese language so perhaps I should explain that I lived in Brazil between the ages of seven and fourteen. I'd been anxious to see the country again.

My family had moved there from France in search of a better climate. Initially we settled in the interior where my parents tried their hand at farming. But my father was actually a metallurgist so we moved on to Brasilia. There was a great need for tradesmen of all kinds during the construction of the new capital so my father opened an engineering workshop there. This was where my brothers and I started to learn about working with steel and welding. After school we often kept busy in the workshop making all sorts of things including, once, a bicycle. However, I must confess that it was very heavy so we didn't ride it very often (my father took the hint though and bought us proper bikes soon after).

I remember having a good time in Brazil. Once we started a small circus, complete with trapeze and tightrope. We became quite good on the trapeze but none of us ever made it across the tightrope. While on the farm we often went bush walking for the day, armed with our best sling shots. Our 'hunting' took us farther and farther away from home in search of 'prey' but if we ever hit a bird with our sling shots we were always sorry and nursed it back to life. Come to think of it, all we ever really got from these safaris was a good scolding from our mother. She was always worried sick about our wanderings in a country that was full of poisonous snakes, scorpions and even the occasional jaguar.

For ex-city kids it was one fantastic experience after another. Each day's exploring brought something new—edible wild fruit, a deserted farm and so on. So despite our mother's warnings our discovery tours continued. But people often underestimate the survival instinct of a child. The bush was actually full of all kinds of dangers and not only from animals. We often came across holes that had been dug deep into the red soil by 'garimpeiros' (topaz prospectors). Just a metre wide and some 20 metres deep, they were often concealed by grass. I don't know how but we never fell in one—kids are survivors.

It may have turned our parents' hair prematurely grey but we had an interesting childhood in Brazil.

I had forgotten much of the language but listening to Brazilian radio for a few days on the way helped a lot and I was able to brush up on my accent. Later this was a bit of a problem though as whenever I asked someone for information or directions they would answer me rapidly in Portuguese, not realising that I wasn't as fluent as my accent suggested.

I had a laugh on the first morning I arrived. I was standing on the pontoon after having tied *Acrohc*. A woman from a nearby Brazilian yacht was rowing toward me in a dinghy. She asked me if I'd seen 'the guy from the small boat'. I told her it was me but she thought I was joking and didn't believe me. In fact she said, 'It can't be you, the boat is Australian'. But after a little while she did pick my slightly 'off' accent and she invited me to her yacht *Jamanxim* for breakfast— what she'd set out to do in the first place.

Her name was Solange and when we got to *Jamanxim* I met Marco. They were from Rio and were off to cruise the world, taking almost the same route as me. They were the kind of people that I take to straight away and I was always pleased to meet up with them in other ports. Marco, a geologist, was full of stories from his ten years in the Amazon jungle searching for minerals. I never tired of listening to his tales of gold miners, Indians and strange animals. He was an exceptional cook too. As for Solange, she quite simply had the travel bug and had already visited most of Europe where she'd learned English and French. All in all the three of us never seemed to stop talking.

My first task after breakfast that morning was to get clearance into the country. I hadn't bothered getting a visa in advance because I'd been told that any yacht calling in at Brazil automatically got permission to stay for six months. No-one, however, had told me that this did not apply to Australians. I was told by the authorities that I had to apply for a visa from outside the country. And Brazil was big! The nearest place was French Guiana, 1,300 miles away. So I accepted the meagre three day permit thinking that at least it was enough time to shop for supplies and repair the headsail which had started to rot.

By Easter Friday I had finished my chores, so with Solange and Marco for company I had a look around the city. On the beach we saw some 'jangadas'. These light sailing rafts are getting scarce because of the shortage of the light timber used in their construction. Now the most popular fishing boats in that area seemed to be made of planks just like any boat except they have a very low freeboard and a large sail on a bamboo mast, jangada style. I don't believe that these boats can be very safe, but given a choice, I'd rather take my chances on one of them than have to tackle the city streets on a regular basis. I was nearly run over twice and later nearly fell down an open manhole. (I was told that they had a birthday party for that manhole when it was 'one year open').

Jangada

Brazil is a strange country. The people are not rich but they don't worry about it. they are very relaxed, except when driving, and only get excited at carnival and soccer time.

Three days wasn't much of a rest after 20 days at sea but that was the law and I had no-one to blame but myself; I should have checked before I got there. Friends told me that there were 'ways' of staying on and I knew the authorities were quite lenient but I didn't want to risk getting into trouble. I wanted to press on anyway. Too bad about the planned visit to the Amazon and too bad about the cute Brazilian girls (a feature of Brazil I hadn't really noticed as a child). But at least I wouldn't be running the risk of getting married there—many a single sailor visiting Brazil has fallen for the beauties—by staying only three days I would be safe!

At 9.00am on Easter Saturday the tide ran out and *Acrohc* went with it. Soon we were out of the river. I could hear the sounds of the Samba coming from the city where it was carnival time once more. But for me it was time to tackle 1,300 miles of coastal sailing—battling ships, lobster pots, muddy waters and terrible humidity. I was tempted to turn back. I pictured myself with a bottle of cachaça in one hand and a girl in the other, dancing in the streets with the crowd. I could have done the Samba until dawn then slept on the beach, forgetting the world. It was time I had a bit of fun so why not??

I was just about to turn around but the white angel kicked the red devil and I came back down to earth. What would my excuse be to the authorities '. . . er . . . I've come back for the carnival?' And besides the current was too strong to sail back. I was out so I stayed out and I left behind the bushwalking and wild fruit country of my youth. Soon I forgot about the carnival and the suntanned 'morenas' and fell asleep. I was very tired; I had not used the three day stopover to catch up on sleep.

The northerly current was strong and the going was good. But the weather was not so nice and it rained for most of the trip. The log reads:

Day 2: Got up at 5.00am very close to a ship. Still tired. One or two knots current. Seen many buoys of lobster posts. Occasional showers. Good radio reception.

Day 4: Slept like a log, only woke up to find it raining.

Day 5: Calm night only one rain storm. Going fast. Eating lots of fruit because all ripened at once. Saw one distant ship and one closer at noon. Nasty weather.

Day 7: Some sun, first for a long time. Got a hair cut. Was cleaning the barnacles, surprised by a squall, lost the brush when in a hurry to get back on board.

I spent quite a lot of time listening to radio broadcasts from Brazil. The news usually reported the grim tidings of a daily average of two deaths from car accidents, half a dozen assaults and two murders.

Then massive rains caused many roads to be washed out and the daily death rate rose as drivers kept running into holes in the roads.

My other occupation was fishing. Once I hooked a beautiful dorado, but this was noticed by a nearby shark and while it was still on the line, the shark helped himself to a couple of mouthfuls. By the time I had pulled the line in there was really only the head of the dorado dangling from the hook, even though I had worked fast. There was only enough meat for one meal left. I was angry with the shark and wanted to spear him but he was much too big. Later that day I caught another dorado but the lure attachment broke and I lost that one as well.

Day 9: Good night with usual blow. Had a bath on deck, shark might still be around. Winds nor-east, lots of waves, overcast. Morale low.

Day 10: Wind force six to seven. Crossed the Equator sometime today. Pilot chart says it should be better weather than that. Horribly hot and humid. No sun.

Day 11: Caught a barracuda on the trawling line at night. Boy, what an ugly fish!

Day 12: Two distant ships. Feeling tired lately as if I was sick, especially at night. Maybe missing a good night's sleep. Found black bugs in the rice and popcorn. (They were only harmless weevils, but I didn't like the look of them in my food.)

Day 13: Not much wind for a change, cleaned the hull with a plastic scraper, sailing twice as fast.

Day 14: Shot a saw-fish, followed boat, too big, broke the line, lost the spear. Ship passed close, no radio reply. No position for sure but near Amazon River, RDF no good, radio no good, too rough for sextant.

That day I got the fright of my life when I looked out through the porthole and saw a big black lump in the water just a few metres ahead of us. Only a whale could look like that and what a place for a whale to sleep! Very quickly I pulled the rudder over and pointed into the wind where Acrohc could turn faster. We made the sharp detour and just missed the tail of the beast. I was halfway through a long sigh of relief when I spotted the trawling line sliding over the back of the whale. The big hook on the end of it would be a rude way to wake a sleeping whale. I could do one of two things, panic or cut the line. Deciding on the latter I grabbed the knife and was ready to cut the line when the whale awoke and moved gently away. I started breathing again a short while later. The whale must have been a little confused as she followed us for about five minutes before gliding away—probably to finish her nap.

Day 15: Winds on the beam, fast going. Waves up to three metres, usual. Forgot Mum's birthday, must have been tired. Saw a yacht for the first time at sea, no radio reply, bully for them. 11.00am, crossed the Atlantic-Trader from Japan, got position fix—60 miles off from my dead reckoning. Saw a few whales, only one came after us for a look.

Day 16: Strange water colour. At noon that day a rough sextant fix showed an odd position. According to the fix, we had made 170 miles in 24 hours; this was far too much. Also, according to my chart there should have been six fathoms of water under us and the echo-sounder wasn't registering anything at all. Where had I gone wrong?

Then I saw a ship so I plugged in the radio's aerial thinking I'd call them up. But as I went to switch the radio on I saw that I hadn't turned it off after the last time I'd used it; the battery pack was flat so I was on my own.

The water was a dark, 'jungle' green and I thought I was entering the shallows that extend 200 miles from the Amazon coast. Later I sighted a narrow stretch of water across my path that was very choppy as though it was very shallow. The depth-sounder wasn't to be trusted so I got back inside, locked the hatch and hoped for the best. But we went through it alright so I assumed that it must have been the meeting point of two currents.

I estimated that we were 250 miles from Cayenne and it was time to head for the coast again. I did so until the sounder showed a depth of 20 metres, then I headed nor'west along the coast. Land was still not in sight.

Day 17: Now 17 metres deep, too rough to open the hatch for radio fix. Still ugly green waters. Land about ten miles according to the depth, later got a fix from beacon in Cayenne.

From there on the weather improved and Acrohc made good progress in the strong current. That night we were ten to 20 miles from the coast and I knew that a few islands without lights lay ahead of us. The water was only 12 metres deep so I decided to anchor for the night. I wanted to get some sleep but I also didn't want to arrive at Cayenne at night as I wanted to be able to check on the currents; the log registered two knots of current where I was anchored.

By next morning I knew what the situation was and that the best time to enter the channel would be about noon. So, I made it to the channel at the right time, easily passing between some nice islands. Everything was going along nicely until a squall blew up. I had to anchor in the mouth of the channel to wait for it to pass. It brought horrible winds, poured rain on us as hard as it could and reduced visibility to a few metres; certainly not pleasant conditions to encounter in a channel.

When the squall had passed we entered the channel itself. It was well marked and was dug out of the mud. That mud! The waters were almost as thick as the mud itself. The shores were mud and the beaches were mud . . . the smell of everything was mud. Horrible!

Halfway up the channel the dredge *Henares* was busy pumping mud and blowing it to the sides of the channel. We had a chat by VHF and I was invited for a cold beer later ashore. *Acrohc* kept going, under sail because the motor wasn't working (again!). This time it was because the fuel was full of water, dirt and rust from the metal petrol tank. It was still the one filled in Cape Town. Then we ran aground or should I say, 'amud'. Surprise, surprise—I could even run aground in a channel built for tankers just because I wasn't exactly between the markers! Mind you the current flowing across the channel brought more mud in than the dredge could pump out. Anyway, I had a mud bath and pushed Acrohc back into the centre of the channel.

Before dark I made a smart manoeuvre under sail and came in nicely alongside the big dock. Pity no-one was watching. The police, however, arrived shortly afterwards and we completed the necessary paperwork. Then it was time to go in search of beer and cigarettes. On my way, I decided that this trying to kick the habit every time I put to sea was stupid if each time I reached a port I made a bee-line for the nicotine. So, I decided to give up after I'd completed the whole journey

There were no shops at the harbour but I found what I wanted on *San Marco*, a Brazilian trading boat.

I was pleased to find that there were a lot of Brazilians in French Guiana which meant that I could practice the language a bit more. It also made up, to a certain extent, for my too short stay in Brazil.

I had my evening meal aboard a French yacht *Le Bleu*. The crew warned me about the water snakes which liked to board yachts at night and about the big spiders and other assorted insects to be found around the place—nice spot for a holiday! But I was amused by some strange looking fish, 'mud-skippers', which swam with their protruding eyes just above the surface. Smart fish because they wouldn't have been able to see a thing in that mud.

I was surprised to find that there were no slipways or careening facilities in the Cayenne harbour. But the dredge *Henares* had just enough room on her foredeck for Acrohc, so her crane plucked my little boat out of the water. They offered this service for a very reasonable fee and also supplied me with paint and two cartons of beer. How could I refuse!

The thick layer of barnacles on Acrohc's hull was replaced by two coats of red, 'dredge' antifouling and next day we left the mud channel. We left one muddy river, sailed for two miles and anchored in another muddy river, the Cayenne River. There I found *Jamanxim* and many other yachts. (It was where I should have arrived first.)

Although it had only been three weeks since I'd seen *Jamanxim* we had a lot to talk about. They only stayed for a week in Cayenne but we were to meet again at our next port of call.

I stayed for three weeks. The town was ugly and the people were not very friendly—they didn't like anyone white, particularly the French. They want independence but the French aren't interested, perhaps because they launch the Ariane space rockets from there. I think the people are being spoiled by the French government so they'll keep quiet but it doesn't really work.

At the anchorage I found *Mallamoc*, the yacht I'd met in South Africa, and her crew took me sightseeing. The countryside was nice with lots of greenery and wildlife. I remember particularly the night we visited a distant beach (muddy of course) where huge 'leatherback' sea-turtles came to lay their eggs. I am very lucky to have seen this phenomenon as these turtles only lay eggs once a year and that beach is their only breeding place. On the way there we passed a river, beautiful because there wasn't so much mud in it. We decided to have a swim in the river after we'd had lunch at a restaurant actually on the banks of the same river. We had to choose from a menu listing such delicacies as snake, beef, lizard and crocodile. 'But,' I asked the waitress 'aren't crocodiles a protected animal?'

'No,' she replied. 'This river is full of them.' So we had crocodile for lunch but no swim afterwards.

On the way to Cayenne I had promised myself a trip up river in a dugout canoe to see the real Amazon jungle in all its reputed glory. But trips with the local tour operators were very expensive so I decided to leave it for my next trip (on which I'd bring my own canoe).

Meanwhile, I'd stayed long enough on land to recover some strength in my legs and be more or less fit to press on. Besides the trip to Panama was only going to be short hops.

François and Ann-Marie of *Mallamoc* invited me for a farewell meal, this time at a French restaurant where the most bizarre item on the menu was only frogs legs. Silvie was three years old by then and beginning to talk better but *Acrohc* was still Little *Mallamoc* to her.

TERN

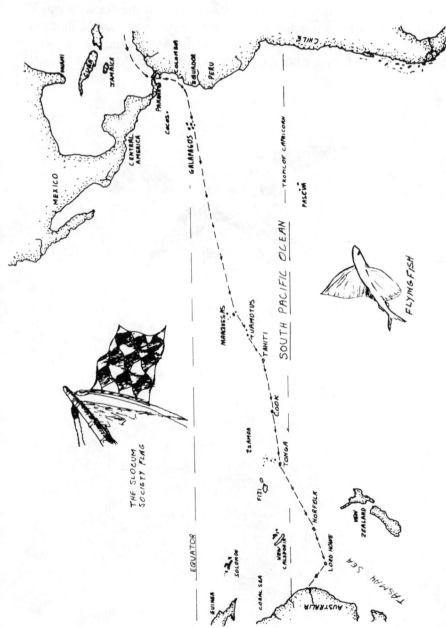

Chapter 9

THE PANAMA CANAL

It was the 11th of May and time to set sail if I wanted to be home for next Christmas. The next stop was to be the Iles Du Salut, only ten miles away.

With strong following winds and current, the ten miles should have been a breeze. But already the hull was so covered in barnacles that our top speed was one knot (the following seas also made steerage almost impossible). It wasn't that the last lot of antifouling was no good it was simply that in the muddy waters of those rivers they'd collect on any hull, regardless of the type of antifouling used. I couldn't see much in that water to clean the hull under way so it would just have to wait until I reached the islands.

So, when I arrived it was the first job I set to after anchoring. The water there was still murky though and I found it difficult to see what I was doing. I was also made to feel even more uncomfortable by the reputation the waters had of being shark infested. Still, it had to be done.

Iles Du Salut is French for Salvation Islands. They were so named because of the refuge they offered to the original settlers of the mainland who were dying from an assortment of diseases. Unfortunately, out of thousands, only a few found refuge on these snake and insect free islands. Later the islands were used by France as prisons, remaining in use until only a few years ago.

Papillon was among those imprisoned. He spent about 20 years on the islands and his book describes the horrors that took place. He finally escaped by taking to the sea, hanging on to a bag of coconuts and drifting to the mainland (. . . and you think I'm crazy!). Strangely though his fame seemed to have escaped the locals who knew little about him except from what they'd read in his book.

Now the islands are more like botanical gardens and if it weren't for the remains of the prisons, it would be hard to believe that hundreds didn't leave the place alive.

In the Iles du Salut trees grow inside the old prison walls

The remains of the prison on the island of St. Joseph have withstood the rigours of time well and are still in quite good condition. There are over 1,000 cells, each the size of a toilet cubicle with iron bars as a roof. But trees do not respect brick and mortar and are growing everywhere, their roots breaking up the foundations of what is left standing. The prisons are no longer the grim harbours of misery and degradation. They still look and feel sinister but they are slowly blending with nature. And tourists like me can wander pleasantly through the ruins and dine in the old mess hall which is now a restaurant.

Two days was enough time to see the small islands and gather some wild fruit to take along. I left on a Tuesday for Tobago to ensure that I wouldn't arrive on a weekend and be charged a large fee for getting clearance into the country. The distance was right for a seven day trip and I anticipated arriving on the following Monday.

The wind and current were favourable and I enjoyed the leg. Admittedly it was a bit windy and the waves were up to four metres high, but at least we were out of the mud and at last sailing in clear blue waters.

The fourth day out a red yacht overtook us. As they passed they said that they were also on their way to Tobago and that they had friends following in another yacht.

On Sunday morning I sighted land, by evening the harbour lights and by late that night *Acrohc* was anchored in Scarborough harbour. 'Good timing,' I said to myself when I found out that Monday was Pentecost, 'I can spend the day cleaning the hull'.

The two yachts which had overtaken me on the way asked me over for coffee. They had arrived on the Saturday, but like me had to wait until Tuesday after the public holiday for clearance. We spent the time nicely, chatting on the boats.

On the Tuesday evening I caught the ferry to Trinidad to call at the Venezuelan consul for a visa and to visit Port of Spain for the day. The people were friendly but not to the same extent as in Tobago—a big city no matter in which country it seems has a strange effect on people.

Back in Tobago I moved to Store Bay, a nicer anchorage on the other side of the island and there met up again with *Jamanxim* and other friends. Store Bay is an ideal spot for diving and spear-fishing, so in the evening we all met on the beach for a flying fish barbecue and I can honestly say that they don't smell bad once cooked.

After five days in Tobago, *Acrohc* found herself sailing towards Margarita, the duty free island port of Venezuela. There I planned to speak Spanish or try to anyway. I'd been listening to their radio station for a few days and I was sure I could make myself understood; after all, if I mixed Italian and Portuguese and spoke with a strange accent I sounded Spanish! The difficult bit was mixing them in the right order.

The morning I left Tobago, while still in the island's lee, *Acrohc* had sailed at better than five knots but as we left the shelter of the island it was business as usual at two to three knots. The only event on that trip was being on a collision course with the cargo ship *Nordic Trader* but luckily we both changed course well in time. However, it was very hazy and this thick, fog-like weather often made visibility limited on that coast.

Two nights at sea later *Acrohc* was anchored for two days in Pampatar, the fishing port of Margarita Island. To my surprise, I found I could manage with Spanish well enough to hold a simple conversation. Once, when I was trying to find Customs, I asked a group of passers-by in my best Spanish for information. 'Señor, digame por favor.' They promptly replied, 'Sorry, we can't speak Spanish, we're French.' So much for my Spanish.

The island seemed dry except for around the seashore. It is extremely tourist oriented, probably because of the low cost of living and many well stocked duty free shops.

Norge and Vincent from the yacht *Supercilious*, which I'd met in South Africa, were waiting for me to arrive at Port Azul. I was eager to get there too. I wanted to refit *Acrohc* most importantly with a new headsail but also with a Satnav (satellite navigator) for the Pacific Ocean leg. The Pacific has a lot of submerged reefs and low islands that are only visible once they're too close. I'd have to be sure of my position at all times and I couldn't rely on the sextant alone. I left Margarita hoping that the trip to Port Azul would only be of two days time like the last one.

The first night a school of dolphins decided that *Acrohc* looked interesting. It was a dark night but the water was very clear and full of fluorescent plankton and the dolphins left bright trails of light behind them as they swam around us. It was beautiful to watch and I got the feeling that the dolphins enjoyed their 'special effects' too. They played for more than two hours and it was just like an underwater fireworks display with the occasional 'bloop' as the dolphins came up for air.

The following few days were hot and humid and I sailed along the coast until the fourth night when I finally saw a light that I assumed was coming from Port Azul. We entered a small marina which didn't look how I'd pictured Port Azul to look but was a perfect place to spend the night.

In the morning I was greeted by the most enchanting sight of a few grass roofed huts nestled near the water and surrounded by garden-like vegetation. In the background were a couple of buildings and behind them a beautiful tree covered mountain. If this was typical of Venezuela then I was in love with it.

After breakfast we set out again along the beautiful coast for Port Azul. We entered another marina but, again, it wasn't Port Azul. There I was told that I was five miles past Port Azul—I had a feeling that good charts of that coast would be helpful. I was at a cute little marina called Marina Mar. Fees for berthing were high there but when the manager saw *Acrohc* he offered me a free pontoon for as long as I wanted it. So, I telephoned Vincent and half an hour later he appeared; it was a happy reunion.

Soon I was at his home in the capital, Caracas. Norge came over and in no time at all I was being introduced proudly to most of their friends. Many, like Norge and Vincent, were of Italian origin and in fact, strangely enough most yacht owners in Venezuela seemed to be Italian. The conversation often came back to, 'You must take *Acrohc* to Port Azul.' I couldn't understand their insistence as there was nothing wrong with where she was. But I felt I should move to Port Azul if only to please everyone, besides, I thought that if they all kept their yachts there it must be for a good reason. I also got the feeling that Norge, who was the commodore at Port Azul, would be happier if I moved.

Two days later I was driven back to *Acrohc*. I wasn't that happy about moving her as it really meant backtracking. But, one hour later when I saw Port Azul from behind the large breakwater wall (which almost hides its small lighthouse), any regrets I had vanished. There were about 200 mostly expensive yachts moored there. There was every facility for overhauling including workshops and a chandler. In addition there were over a hundred apartments in half a dozen or so blocks, a cinema, bowling alley, and a gym. There were soccer grounds, tennis courts and all sorts of other sporting facilities, different types of restaurants and even a disco. I was looking at a complete holiday village in itself. I was given a royal welcome and, despite it being a private club, I was able to use all the facilities— maybe because I knew the right people! Mind you, cruising yachties generally seemed to be welcomed and well treated, all that is except the French, who had a bad reputation (one had once been found washing his sails in one of the swimming pools). *Acrohc* was the main attraction at the resort. She was given a nice place to stay where pretty young girls could come and visit her and she was also given new antifouling and new sails. In Venezuela sail material is a scarce commodity but Juan, one of *Supercilious*' crew, had found the main of a starboat and had cut a genoa and staysail out of it. He had enough left over to make a sail bag too.

I was invited to sleep on *Supercilious* whenever I was at the club. I accepted as *Acrohc* was too popular for me to get a good, uninterrupted night's sleep. But most of the time I was a guest of Norge or Vincent in Caracas.

One night at a small ceremony I was made a 'Brother of the Coast'. This association was started in Chile about five centuries ago by ex-buccaneers. Since then it has expanded all around the world, but is best known in Europe. A proposed Brother has to be nominated at one of their meetings and if his nomination is successful, he's in. There are no membership fees or paperwork, just how you would imagine a pirate's association to be. They've retained the fraternity but not the pirating (perhaps a pity!) and the main requirements are to be a good seaman and to obey a set of rules. For example, 'Thou shall not desire your brother's yacht nor his sails or motor.' We have our own flag so that we can recognise each other. I was proud to be selected and promised to honour the Brotherhood.

Back at the club *Acrohc* and I were given a party. I had to talk about my trip and answer questions which I managed quite well in my broken Spanish although, of course, Norge was there to help. I really enjoyed myself and we all had a good laugh with the rum punch helping to release my Spanish.

Among other things I had to replace was a camera. Mine had become very corroded and I was looking for another. I happened to mention it to Vincent in passing and he immediately offered me just the camera I needed, a water-proof one. I also needed a Super-8 camera to record a bit more of my trip for friends at home. Hectore (a Brother of the Coast), gave me one.

Apparently there weren't any Satnavs in Venezuela but I told this to my brother Henry (my real brother) and he sent me one from Brisbane as a present from him and my other two brothers. They sent it to Bonaire which was to be my next port of call as it had a more reliable mail system.

All the while I shopped around for supplies, which I found to be cheap, and enjoyed touring the countryside. Venezuela is full of green mountains and its capital, Caracas, is a large busy city nestled 1,000 metres high among them. Compared to the hot and humid climate of the coast, Caracas is rather cold. There is an impressive metro there which is new and kept immaculately clean and above it thousands of cars crowd the streets—far too many for a city that cannot expand because of the surrounding mountains.

The wealthy have a very nice lifestyle and the standard of living for the working class is average. But when Venezuela was richer, at the time when oil prices reached their height, illegal migrants from neighboring countries poured in and these people are not doing so well now. The contrast can be clearly seen in the city where lots of 'Ranchitos' (houses cheaply built by the poor people on any spare land) have appeared between the luxurious buildings. About 30 per cent of Caracas is made up of Ranchitos. There are far too many for the government to take care of properly and this was especially the case when I was there (which was during the oil crisis). Nonetheless, the country is beautiful and the people are nice, especially the girls! I certainly didn't regret staying there for the two months.

On many occasions I was taken on excursions into the countryside and one memorable week was spent at the nearby atoll of Los Roques on Vincent's yacht. The beautiful coral I saw there reminded me of the Barrier Reef but on a much smaller scale.

On Monday the 21st of July *Acrohc* was ready to leave. The Satnav was waiting in Bonaire, the shopping was done and I had new sails. I said my good byes to everyone and sailed away once more.

The new staysail worked well but there was too much wind for comfort and the rough seas claimed another bucket from the deck. I must admit that getting used to being back at sea wasn't easy.

Thanks to the strong winds I arrived in Bonaire too early, at night. I anchored in the lee of the island and the following morning sailed to a small marina. There I picked up the Satnav and installed it in a recess into the side of the bulkhead. To protect it from the humidity I covered the front of it with a clear perspex door. Friends I'd met in Port Azul helped me tilt *Acrohc* over so I could fix the aerial to the top of the mast, then I was ready for a few beers at the hotel next door during the happy hour.

There wasn't much to do in Bonaire. It was dry and very windy so it was not very appealing.

Three days later I was back at sea on the way to Panama. That evening I sailed past the island of Curaçao where lay the capital of the Netherlands Antilles (the semi-independent Dutch colony that includes Curaçao, Bonaire and Aruba). Aruba, I have been told is the nicest of the three and is famous for its casino and diving.

This leg was horrible though. The winds blew invariably at 20 to 30 knots and the big waves, constantly crashing over *Acrohc*, took another bucket. If you can't help wondering how I managed without a toilet bucket, here for your enlightenment is the procedure: First I'd make sure there wasn't a mean wave heading for us. Then I'd quickly open the hatch and nip outside, careful to close the hatch after me (the hatch was also fitted with an outside lock). When I'd finished the job at hand I'd quickly get back inside and dry myself. It was never pleasant but it at least I'd get a wash from the waves at the same time.

One good thing about the trip was that the Satnav proved its worth. I didn't need to open the hatch to get a sextant or RDF reading any longer. All I did was turn on the machine, punch a few buttons and soon I'd know where I was. It meant that at night I could sail close to islands safely and without having to worry. It was not a cheap thing to have on board but for safety and peace of mind there was nothing better. I'd met more than one sad sailor who'd lost his boat because he hadn't known exactly where he was.

On the sixth night, *Acrohc* was shaken by a severe storm. It lasted for the next two days and brought some of the worst conditions I'd yet sailed in. The strong winds and the swell which grew to more than five metres high made it extremely difficult to steer a straight course. I wasn't amused by the waves pushing us over until the mast hit the water and my supplies looked as though they'd been through a cement

The satellite navigator is housed in the bulkhead. It replaced the sextant in the box above. In the top centre we can see part of the inside tiller system. On the right is the depth sounder that never recovered from the wave that got in.

mixer. I spent most of the time trying to hang on, sometimes losing my grip as a particularly vicious wave hit us.

The good thing, though, was that we were travelling much faster than I'd estimated and I wanted to get out of those waters as quickly as possible as I didn't want any pirates to find us. These pirates hunt up and down the Colombian coast, after any sort of boat that can be used for drug running. The crews of their victim boats are given to the sharks. Most yachts give this section of the coast a wide berth. In fact insurance companies don't give coverage to yachts intending to sail there.

The pirates probably wouldn't have been interested in smallfry like *Acrohc* but nevertheless I stayed 60 miles off the coast. Who would be silly enough to sail in those conditions anyway!? The good thing

140

about the strong winds was that I could find out how good my new staysail was. The reason I'd installed it was so that I could have a small sail area as low as possible during storms, which I couldn't have with a furling genoa. But this new sail once it was up couldn't be reduced without going on deck. I also found that it was still too big. (Later I had it recut to a smaller size so that it was just enough to cope with storms.)

By the eighth day the storm had eased and I could finally cook a hot meal without spilling too much of it. I even risked opening the hatch for a couple of hours. From that day on the weather was more reasonable, with only the odd squall.

I should mention at this point the river of floating junk brought out to sea by the surface currents, a hundred miles before Panama. I wasn't surprised as I'd been told about it previously but the variety of the mainly plastic and timber rubbish was amazing. There was everything from toothbrushes to telephone poles in one continuous stream of debris. (I hoped to spot one of my buckets but was unlucky). It took me half a day to get across it. I wish people would stop dumping rubbish at sea before it's too late.

I had also been warned about the ten metre swell just off the Panama coast. This swell is probably caused by the Caribbean Sea coming to a dead end.

As I got closer to the Panama Canal, the traffic intensified and I started to worry about the number of ships passing us. At night I was using the strobe light tied onto the boom but on the last night before reaching Panama I was getting up at intervals of 15 minutes. Even doing this I sometimes found us uncomfortably close to a ship.

On the eleventh day I sighted the stormy land of Panama. The skies were full of black clouds, thunder, lightning and, as I'd been warned, rain. Later I found that this weather was the norm in Panama. The country itself was just as ugly and everything was very expensive.

We arrived on the 5th of August at an anchorage called the 'Flats'. There I cleared with Customs without going ashore. Two hours later

I tied up at the yacht club at a cost of $15.00—Panama used U.S. dollars. (They call their money 'Balboa' but the funny thing is they don't print any!)

I needed an entry stamp on my passport and eventually found the immigration officers in the bar. Then I went to their main office so I could get a visa; cost, $10.00. Next I was issued with a cruising permit by an ugly, illtempered lady. She wanted photocopies of everything and exact change of $10.90. I then had to show my visa to the immigration people and I thought on my way back to the bar that at least they were easy to find . . . at the bar!

That was clearance. Now to get through the Panama Canal . . !

The next day I made an appointment with the 'Admeasurer' for the following morning. The Admeasurer is the person who measures the inside and outside of boats so that the cost of the passage through the canal can be worked out. He didn't turn up at the agreed time so I made another appointment for the next day. This time he did turn up. He measured *Acrohc* and as they could only 'swindle' $1.80 per ton, he decided that she weighed two tons instead of half a ton. I was happy to only have to pay $2.60 for the passage until I found out the charge for his services, $40.00!

Then it was off to see the Canal Harbour Master to organise the actual crossing. *Acrohc* could not carry the required pilot and four line-handlers, so we decided that I should find a yacht that was also crossing and arrange to tie *Acrohc* onto her for the crossing of the locks. I would still cross Gatun Lake (part of the Canal) under my own power though, so I still required a pilot.

They were considerate enough to select a really light pilot for us with the added advantage that 'she' was cute! I paid the $55.00 crossing fee and went back to the club where I met Juan. He owned the yacht *Castelao* and volunteered to have *Acrohc* tied to her side for the crossing.

Juan was a fun loving Spaniard who'd bought his yacht in Panama to do some commercial fishing and was crossing the Canal to try his luck on the Pacific side of Panama. Actually, I refer to Juan as a Spaniard simply because it was easy to imagine him clad in the armour of a 16th century Conquistador. I don't know what gave me that impression but I suspect it was just the way he spoke of his native Spain.

After a beer we decided that to simplify matters *Castelao* should also tow *Acrohc* across the Lake, so we went back to the Harbour Master's office. The towing license cost $5.00. We arranged for the pilots to meet us at 6.00am on the following Monday for the crossing.

Monday 6.00am came but no pilots. I later found out that the time had been changed to 8.00am which explained why the pilots turned up at 9.00am! Well, it's a hot country and it's difficult to be on time—I understand that!

So, at 9.00am my pilot embarked and we motored to the Flats where *Castelao* was waiting. My pilot didn't need much persuading to do the trip on *Castelao* in more comfort and I didn't mind—they'd switched pilots on me—this one was not a girl. I didn't need a pilot anyway.

Three and a half miles later we were in front of the first lock's gates. There are two canals, side by side, and we entered the lefthand one behind a huge tanker. We tied *Acrohc* securely to *Castelao* while the big doors slowly closed behind us. The linesmen on the sides of the canal threw us the four 'monkey fists' which our lines were hoisted with and *Castelao* was secured.

When the doors were closed water started flooding the lock. It came through big holes in the bottom and this had the effect of making the entire lock seem like a spa bath. It took about ten minutes of this to lift us about ten metres to the height of the next lock and we shortened the securing lines as the water rose. As the gates to the next lock opened, the tanker ahead of us caused a good deal of turbulence but we carefully motored along behind. Then the whole thing started over with everyone busy pulling on lines to keep us centered and me trying to calm *Acrohc* who wanted to do her own thing.

The next set of gates opened onto the freshwater Gatun Lake, 25 metres above sea level. We secured the tow ropes between *Castelao* and *Acrohc* and motored peacefully through the beauty of the 23 miles of artificially flooded tropical forest. Before long a storm blew up, complete with thunder, lightening and rolling waves. I locked myself in the cabin but despite the heavy rain I could still see *Castelao* ahead of me and the odd channel buoy through the portholes.

My outboard was running to help against the strong wind and all I had to do was steer *Acrohc* along behind *Castelao*. I was sure the two pilots on board *Castelao* knew the way so my only fear was of the tow line snapping. We were motoring along at five knots and every time *Castelao* hit a wave she lost speed as her bow lifted, then she'd pick up speed as she ran down the other side of it. *Acrohc* being pulled along behind had no option but to plough straight through the waves. It wasn't any wonder that I couldn't undo the tow line afterwards.

Two hours later the wind eased and the storm disappeared. I found out later that *Castelao's* crew had followed the channel by guess work—not only was the visibility bad but they hadn't been able to look ahead for the blinding rain that was driving into their faces.

If that kind of weather is the norm for this region it is little wonder that the canal took ten years to build and cost so many lives.

After another two hours of lake sailing we entered Galliard Cut, a portion of the canal that had been cut through eight miles of rock and shale. Then we were ready for the three down locks that would take us back to sea level and the Pacific.

These locks were easier to manoeuvre because the water was being drained out instead of being pumped in and there was no turbulence especially with the tanker having gone on ahead. By the time we had reached the first lock we were joined by another yacht so the three of us were tied alongside each other looking somewhat like a trimaran. We were lowered onto the smaller Miraflore Lake which is just one mile long and from there we entered the last two locks. We had reached the Pacific after travelling 50 miles of canal. (Maybe I should explain that the Atlantic and Pacific are not at different levels. The locks are just there for ships to travel overland and cross the lakes.)

By five o'clock that afternoon we had finished our celebrations of the crossing and without pause started celebrating our arrival at the Pacific Ocean. We dropped our pilots off at the Balboa Yacht Club and had a few more celebratory drinks at the bar. Later we had dinner on *Castelao* and continued the celebrations! It was midnight when I finally found a mooring for the night. This trip could kill me alright, but it wouldn't be the sea!

But these celebrations were special for me as I'd left another ocean behind me. Now I was in the Pacific and well on the way home. I'd sailed two thirds of the way around the world and it felt great. I often thought about the yellow smoke flare that I'd throw in the water when my circumnavigation was complete. That moment was getting closer. And I often wondered what I'd remember most about the trip. Maybe I'd feel sorry that it ended despite the sometimes hard going.

The following morning I visited the Balboa Yacht Club as I'd planned to stay for a couple of weeks. I was given a piece of paper and when I recovered from the shock of seeing the prices they charged I told the man what he could do with his list and motored to Taboga, a small island a few miles away. Taboga had a small bay where I could anchor for free. It also had a ferry which I was told would take me to the town for a dollar a trip.

It turned out that the ferry ride was two dollars each way but the island was nice and the ferry fare was compensated by the fact that on Taboga *Acrohc* was out of reach of most of the famous Panamanian thieves—I say most as I had to bribe the ferryman to let me carry fuel across from the mainland!

I met a few nice yachties on Taboga. Magnus and Dora were a retired couple from Iceland cruising on their yacht, *Dora*. They told me that although most of Iceland's 250,000 inhabitants still lived off the sea, their yacht was the only one being taken around the world.

Actually I'd met Magnus and Dora at the Flats when we were doing our paperwork there. I'd been their interpreter in Panama on many shopping trips. They didn't really need an interpreter though and managed to get their point across quite well. Since their retirement they'd been cruising around just enjoying themselves, not missing their homeland's weather at all! I really enjoyed their company and together we saw many a bottle of brandy emptied.

I also met Didier, another solo traveller, who'd arrived direct from Tahiti. I volunteered to act as one of his linehandlers for his crossing of the canal. There was no storm during that trip so I could enjoy the scenery.

However, despite the friends I made and the stormy beauty of some of the countryside, I swore that I'd never set foot in Panama again. If it wasn't storms and heavy rain, it was muggings. Anyone looking slightly like a tourist was at risk.

TUNA

Chapter 10

From Humboldt To Hula-Hula

Acrohc and I had to be well prepared for the next leg to Galapagos. We had to be ready and able to fight our way against current and winds for 850 miles. If all went well the best time in which I could hope to reach Galapagos was one month; with bad conditions, two to three months. And, if everything went wrong, I would have to consider turning back.

I knew also that I'd only be allowed to stay there for three days—a longer stay would have taken nine months to organise and that was by bribing the right people—and as I didn't know what supplies would be available there I had to have enough to last for the duration of the following leg just in case. And it was 3,000 miles to the next port!

On the 2nd of November, 1986, I lifted anchor and Acrohc headed southwest. I left early that day and as it was raining, I had to try to keep a look out for large floating debris as well as ships from inside the cabin. After hitting the second floating log though, I decided to stop for the night at one of the islands of Las Perlas, an island group still inside the Gulf. There I spent the night anchored in a small bay.

I'd heard of the islands from a cruising couple who had chosen to settle on one of them. Most were deserted but each had plenty of wildlife and vegetation, good fishing and lots of peace and quiet—the perfect setting for anyone looking for a Robinson Crusoe lifestyle. There are lots of this type of island around Panama and all around the world for that matter, if anyone is interested.

I lifted anchor the next morning and continued on my way. That day I encountered a leaping manta ray, two seasnakes, lots of dolphins, three canoes being paddled between islands, a large ship, a couple of tuna boats and lots of floating logs and other debris. I had been wise not to sail through there at night.

I also trimmed my beard and gave myself a haircut. I confess that it was a bit of a rough job, very short and uneven, but it would grow back by the time I'd see someone again. In the meantime it was cooler and easier to wash with the limited supply of freshwater. Actually I used very little fresh water for washing, usually shampooing with saltwater and sometimes using only half a glass of freshwater to rinse the salt out.

By nightfall we were out of the Gulf and I thought we were out of reach of Panama's storms. But, as a send off, we were hit by an electrical storm, windless but with lots of rain and for hours there were bolts of lightening all around us. The lightening was so bright that I had to protect my eyes from the constant flashes. I couldn't look outside but I could tell that the bolts were striking very close to *Acrohc* by the crackling of the electrical charges which made the air in the cabin tremble. It was very impressive.

I was a little worried about *Acrohc* actually being struck as there was a good chance that all my electrical equipment would go berserk, even if they weren't hooked up to the battery. My beautiful Satnav, for example, wouldn't have stood a chance and its aerial on the top of the mast was the perfect conductor.

Theoretically I was safe. Apparently the charge from a bolt of lightening that hits a boat is channelled harmlessly into the water via the mast and rigging and the boat itself. But who believes in theory?

A little past midnight I lay on my bunk trying to get some sleep, making sure that I wasn't touching anything metallic by padding the side of the bunk with blankets—I wasn't about to leave anything to theory. I was soon asleep despite the noise and by morning all was peaceful as though nothing had happened. We had got through it untouched and I am glad to say that was the one and only time I encountered an electrical storm.

On the third day I used the motor again to make headway. The wind finally came up on the fourth day. Unfortunately it was a headwind and it lasted the whole of that leg, its direction never changing more than 20 degrees.

The days passed with the annoying monotony of *Acrohc* hitting a small wave and losing precious speed, then recovering and picking up a little before she hit the next wave. Each time she hit a wave the water became white with foam which was nice to look at but, as many of the waves actually broke over the cabin, I could open the hatch only at the risk of getting everything wet. This went on for the next 15 days.

The heeling degree was also uncomfortable and we were heeling at 30 to 40 degrees for most of the time to get the best possible speed. The deck was so often wet or underwater that weeds started to grow on it!

We sailed in long, boring tacks; one day west, one day south. We were only making one to two knots, just enough to make some headway. During that time of sailing along the Colombian coast we stayed about 50 miles out to sea, close enough to escape the current from the south but far enough to avoid falling prey to the pirates who also infest this coast of Colombia.

Thanks to the Satnav I was able to work out my position accurately twice a day and keep a close check on what the current was up to. If I'd have still been using the sextant I would have been in serious trouble as the sun only shone for a couple of hours in the entire 15 day period.

Because of *Acrohc's* motion, cooking was reduced to one fast daily meal. During the voyage I had always made sure that I had a minimum of one hot meal per day no matter what the weather was like and this had almost always been possible, even if I had to keep balancing the pot. However, I started to think that some strange forces were working against me. First it was the methylated spirits. My latest batch turned out to be 20 degrees weaker than usual and I had to use a lot more as it didn't burn so well, so it nearly ran out. Then the handle of my only cooking pot came off while I was washing it over the side. This left me stupidly holding the handle while the pot disappeared into the brine. Not discouraged by this I cut an old milk tin down and riveted the handle of the old pot onto it.

Next I noticed that my newly installed burner (that I'd kept as a spare) had started to leak internally and was slowly filling up with alcohol. I discovered this when I lit it one day and the flame got big enough to cook a meal for an entire battalion, even charcoaling it in the process. All I could do was shield the tank with a dish to protect it from excess heat and hold an upside-down pot over the flame to contain it until all the alcohol burned up. I would have used the extinguisher but I was already using the other hand to stop myself from being thrown about; I simply ran out of hands.

While I was waiting for the alcohol to burn out I remembered my last brush with fire and said to myself, 'If the tank gets too hot it could blow up. Will I be as lucky this time?' The situation now was different; I had time to think and see the danger . . . and I had time to feel frightened. But my luck held and a few minutes later the flame died down. As soon as the burner had cooled I replaced it with the old one which I had luckily kept.

I persisted with the cooking and had varying success, but I never went without my daily hot meal.

By the ninth day out the weather had cleared and the wind eased enough so that I could wash some underwear in saltwater and take a bath. There was no jumping into the sea though; we were sailing in the Humboldt current which comes direct from the South Pole.

I simply sat on deck with a bucket of water and a bar of soap. (Are you surprised that I still had a bucket?)

That afternoon I sat outside with a warm can of beer and some peanuts to enjoy the faint sun. What luxury. And that night I got my first good night's sleep for a long time.

Three days of relatively smooth sailing had gone by but I could tell that something was wrong. We were losing speed each day and gradually the log stopped registering altogether. This usually meant barnacles. I wasn't looking forward to getting into that cold water to clean the hull and there were still a few waves around that would make it a hard job but it had to be done—I had to at least check the hull.

After I furled the sails I put on my diving mask and braced myself for the plunge . . . I didn't jump. There was a small whale a couple of metres behind us and although they didn't hurt people (and this one wasn't even a killer whale) I just wasn't prepared to go swimming with it! Also, in my defence, when I say 'small whale' I mean 'small for a whale'; it was still twice the length of *Acrohc*. It played around for five minutes or so, at times coming under the hull. It had the curiosity of a three year old child. Finally it swam away, probably having been called by its mother.

When I eventually jumped into the water what I saw horrified me. The hull was absolutely covered with gooseneck barnacles in clumps as big as a fist. No wonder we had been sailing like a log.

I scraped most of them off but couldn't finish the job because of the cold and *Acrohc's* wild motion without sails to steady her so I left the rest for a calmer day. However, what I'd done improved our speed quite a bit and that day we made our best run of the leg, 60 miles directly towards Galapagos.

We'd been sailing for 24 days and we could have made the remaining distance in three more days if the wind had held but sadly it weakened and Acrohc just wasn't able to sail close to the wind and point well. I tried to use the outboard but, as usual, it refused to start.

I tried to find the cause of the problem by leaning over the back of the boat to work on the motor but it was impossible to do much that way. It was heart breaking to be sitting there at the mercy of the current which was always waiting for an opportunity to take back the precious miles we'd gained inch by inch.

Two days later the wind blew a little stronger but the hull was again so dirty that *Acrohc* could point even less. It was upsetting enough to make me lean over the side to scrape away those freeloading barnacles. But being constantly hit by waves, I eventually had to give it up and get back in the cabin to warm up and dress the sores I'd got from lying on the deck.

I just had to be patient and wait for a change of wind; 30 degrees either way would have been enough. My only consolation was the fact that we were at least making a few miles a day.

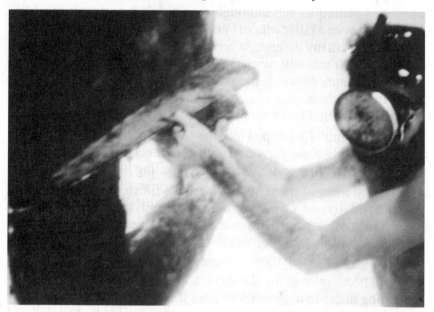

The hull often needed scrubbing en route to remove weeds and barnacles. (This photo was taken at anchorage)

We continued fighting our way south and on the 28th day we crossed the Equator. I didn't celebrate—how could I with the current against us, the wind no help at all, the motor not working and those blasted barnacles . . ! I damned the lot, not forgetting the stupid persistent waves.

I was sick of leaning at 40 degrees all the time, stuck in the cabin and permanently cold. Would I never get there? The situation wasn't just bad, it was disgusting—I was only 40 miles from land but at the rate we were going it would take six days to reach port!

The next day was even worse. *Acrohc* was at exactly the same position she'd been two days earlier. I tried laughing it off but all I could manage was a strangled choking sound, more like crying; something had to be done! I headed east for a couple of days, sailing as close to the light wind as I could, to see what would happen.

October 5th, my birthday, came and went. It was the usual cheerless cold and cloudy day and, as when I'd crossed the Equator, I was not in the mood for celebrating, despite my sneaking suspicion that we were slowly getting somewhere.

The battery was as low as I was feeling. The solar panel hadn't had any proper sunshine since we'd left Panama and even though I'd been using the kerosene lamp for lighting and had lately only been turning the Satnav on once a day for a fix, battery power was really low.

Two days of westerly sailing took us to the 34th day. That day the Satnav said our position was only 17 miles east of San Cristobal. I couldn't see the island because of the fine rain. But knowing it was so close made me feel better despite the fact that we still had another day's sailing to reach our anchorage; the harbour was on the other side of the island.

By evening we were close enough to have a really good look at the coast. I drank to the sight of land with the same sort of relief as I imagine someone who'd been adrift in a liferaft for a month would feel as the sea-rescue boat roared up to them. But when *Acrohc* got too close for comfort, I tacked away from land and prepared to spend the last night of that trip at sea.

I went to sleep and woke up when I found out that Donald Duck could write a cheque; it was midnight and time to turn again to head back to the island. Then I went back to sleep. A square- rigger sailed past, followed by a steam ship with Donald on it. It was two o'clock, time to wake up and check our position. I found we were ten miles off the coast which was too close. We headed back out to sea and I slept again.

When morning came we sailed happily towards the harbour. The motor, which had decided to work, helped in the light wind. I knew it would take about half a day to get in and I was in a hurry to get through the shallow reef before dark. We made it easily. I was relieved to have ended that trip. It had been the section I'd feared the most.

As I passed the reefs I recognised *Dora* at anchor in the bay so I tied to them and went on board for a reunion. We were happy to meet again and had a lot to talk about and a lot to drink. I believe we also had supper that night!

*****

I had three days to prepare for the next leg. Most importantly I had to find more methylated spirits for the stove, a new cooking pot and some more supplies. I found most of what I needed in the village where there were a few small shops and restaurants, but methylated spirits wasn't available. All I could get was one litre from the Navy Base hospital, from the same people who had charged me US$59.00 for a three day harbour fee—a lot of money for just an anchorage and not much time to visit.

However, I found the time to see the interior of the island from the cab of an old hire truck, with Magnus and Dora for company and a dozen or so kids who came along for the ride. Our tour took us to a lake inside the crater of an extinct volcano that had filled with water.

Its diameter was about a mile and it was the only supply of freshwater for the island. Apparently it was a great find for the discoverers of the island, who had actually run out of water before reaching the islands. After a refreshing walk among the clouds around the old volcano, we drove down to the beach to see the seals sunbathing on the rocks, passing the airport on the way. The seals, locally known in Spanish as 'sea wolves', were supposedly fairly tame and used to being photographed but I still approached them with caution; their head looks like a dog's and their teeth are just as sharp. After taking a few snapshots we headed back to the village, stopping on the way to chase iguanas. These lizards are really prehistoric looking, even uglier than the lizards back home.

In the Galapagos Islands, most creatures have evolved quite differently from elsewhere on earth because of its unique climate and isolation. In fact, the islands themselves are unique with a lot of indigenous flora and fauna, although some of it drifted there with the help of the Humboldt current from the South American continent.

There are strange contrasts, like cactus growing on desert-like volcanic ground with penguins wandering around nearby. And there are unique animals in addition to the iguanas, like cormorants. There, because, it was best to swim for food, they had forgotten how to fly. Then there is the Galapago, a huge tortoise that has adapted itself to each of the islands. In fact, their evolution is so finely tuned to their environment that each crater on each of the islands has its own tailor-made species of tortoise to suit the differing vegetation.

The second largest crater in the world is also to be found in the region. Not all of the volcanoes are extinct though and only a few years ago one came to life on Santa Isabella.

People live on the islands despite the rough terrain. Many are the descendants of convicts that were brought there from Ecuador but lately tourism has attracted more mainlanders looking for work. They were nice people though and not all were interested only in the almighty dollar.

Too soon my time there was up which was a shame as I was just beginning to get acquainted with the locals. I learned that the only way to really appreciate a place was by getting to know the people there; that way I could get a better understanding of their culture and see a lot more than just the standard tourist areas.

Acrohc was ready for another long trip at sea, but I wasn't! I wanted to have a longer rest and see some more of the islands. So, the authorities thought that I was going straight to the Marquesas Islands but I intended to stop in Santa Isabella with *Dora* for a few days.

We left at the same time to make the 120 mile trip. *Dora* motored there overnight but because *Acrohc* was slower I stopped for a night at the island of San Salvador where I found a snug little bay, out of sight of the authorities. I had time to swim ashore before dark to look for some of the strange animals but apart from cacti, iguanas and a few birds there wasn't much to see near the beach. I wasn't prepared to go further inland as the ground was difficult to walk on. San Salvador is the island on which the Darwin Centre is working to preserve the fauna. I'd have liked to have visited the centre but to go there would have meant another $59.00 harbour fee.

The next morning I continued on to Santa Isabella, the largest island of the group. It boasts the most fauna and also has the most live volcanos. I found the small bay on the north of the island where *Dora* was anchored without any trouble. I had been told that the authorities never went there because of its distance from the main town. The bay was surrounded by rugged, volcanic outcrops with only cactus struggling to grow here and there. In the background was a big tree-covered volcano that probably was home to lots of animals, however, it was much too far to walk over the rough lava. I had been told that there were lots of animals on the other side of the island and a nice anchorage but going there was, of course, out of the question for we 'illegals'.

If we'd wanted to do the sightseeing thing properly we would have had to go to the harbour at the south of the island and take a guide on board for the day. The main reason for the guides is so that they can make sure that there is no ecological disturbance and that no foreign flora or fauna are introduced. Flora and fauna even from neighbouring islands are considered foreign and potentially damaging to the delicate ecological balance of each of the islands. I have always been very careful not to vandalise nature and understood the reason for a guide but to take one on board *Acrohc* was out of the question . . .well, if there'd been 'guidesses' perhaps I could have found room . . !

Anyway, we limited ourselves to jumping across the lava and watching cormorants swimming after fish. The cormorants didn't seem to mind and were as curious about us as we were of them. None of the animals on the Galapagos Islands are afraid of man as there are no predators on the islands. In the old days ships used to load their holds with thousands of live tortoises which were in demand for their meat and oil. They were easy to catch and were stacked live on top of each other for the trip.

Now all the islands are national parks, a small move to repair the damage caused in earlier times, and the tortoise population is slowly recovering.

WANDERING ALBATROSS

We stayed in that rather rough and windy anchorage for two days. I had time to clean *Acrohc's* hull and I was helped by some parrot fish; they ate the barnacles and I cleaned off the weeds. I couldn't stay in the water for more than a half an hour at a time though because of the cold but I still managed to dive for some 'conchas' at lunch. At night a lobster fishing boat anchored next to us. They were out of cigarettes and I love lobster so we made a fair swap with them and had a lovely dinner that night aboard *Dora.*

We liked the place—for Magnus and Dora it was just like Iceland (cold and volcanic). But I preferred coconut-tree-lined beaches with colourful coral, a bright sun and girls dancing the hula-hula. I didn't have far to go to find it; my next port of call, the Marquesas, were a mere 2,750 miles to the west. It was the longest leg of the entire trip but with good winds and favourable currents I'd make it within two months of easy sailing.

Dora and *Acrohc* left before noon one day after we had a short battle to recover their respective anchors from the rocky bottom. We were off again and this time with good wind and the right current. It wasn't long before *Dora* became a speck on the horizon ahead then disappeared altogether.

Six days went by and it was easy going except there was little sun and the wind was blowing a bit too strongly. The battery had recovered somewhat though and I started using the Satnav again.

I wasn't surprised to learn that we'd travelled 550 miles in six days. The Humboldt Current, like the wind, travels up the South American coast, turns in a wide arc which passes Galapagos, and keeps going northwest, then turns directly west. I was now following the arc of the current and was being taken more or less directly to the Marquesas.

Fishing proved fruitless and on the tenth day I very quickly retrieved the line when I saw the dark shape of a whale next to *Acrohc*. From then on I did no more fishing unless I could stay out and keep an eye on what was around. I was always worried that I'd hook a dolphin and I certainly didn't want to upset a whale by putting a hook through its nose. Too many boats had been sunk in those waters by killer whales and although I was sure *Acrohc* wouldn't sink I didn't want to be rammed by one.

Some days later (possibly the 15th but it doesn't matter, the days were all the same) the weather was decidedly nicer and the wind more reasonable so I thought I'd better check on the barnacle situation. Yep, it was bad alright. The antifouling I'd got in Venezuela was much worse than the others I'd used. This time there were two types of barnacles; a long one called a gooseneck and the usual cone shaped ones.

The gooseneck attaches itself to the hull with a strong but supple muscle which extends outside its shell. They are the hardest to clean off. The common cone shaped barnacle can be scraped off quite easily but they are hard and the tip of the cone is quite sharp. When in the water cleaning I often got nasty cuts from brushing against the hull. Those cuts can turn into coral ulcers, also called tropical ulcers. The ulcers are caused by a coral polyp getting into the cut and growing in the moisture and warmth our bodies provide. They are very common in tropical islands and very difficult to get rid of, even with the help of antibiotics. I was lucky never to be badly infected; perhaps it was because I was always extremely careful to thoroughly clean and disinfect any cuts I got.

I made a good job of cleaning the hull of barnacles. I only ended up with a couple of scratches but I was stung by jellyfish in two places: on my cheek and where I should have been wearing shorts! But the half an hour in the water was time well spent as, with a light wind, *Acrohc* was again smoothly gliding through the water at the dizzying speed of three knots.

The days went by slowly though and I was a bit bored. I got a sore bottom from sitting all the time but apart from that, all was well.

By the 17th day the weather was still improving. I checked our position and found that we'd travelled another 480 miles. The following day *Acrohc* crossed the halfway point that I'd marked on the chart. Halfway was always something to look forward to as from then on it was 'down hill'.

By the 23rd day the weather was really good and I put the blankets out to dry with a sigh of relief at the thought of not having to sleep with damp ones. This was the third day running I'd been able to keep the hatch open, even though the winds were coming directly from behind us and we were rolling a bit. I'd still not caught anything on my trawling line but it didn't matter—I had plenty of food and only a thousand miles to go.

The days went on. Only 600 miles to go, then 300. All was well although the wind insisted on picking up at night and this interfered with my sleep, but I spent the days lazily enough for this not to be a problem. I wrote, drew boat plans or just sat and thought—particularly doing a lot of the latter. I often caught myself thinking aloud or having long conversations with myself. I think it helped keep my vocal chords in shape. When things went well I even sang, something I only do when I'm alone (I know how horrible I sound).

One evening when I was preparing to make a soup for dinner I heard a loud bang on the hull followed by a lot of splashing. I was sure we'd hit a sleeping whale and leapt outside to apologise before it got too upset. But it wasn't a whale, just a tuna nearly the size of one. It was leaping around like crazy trying to catch one of the small fish that were swimming close to *Acrohc* for protection. One little fish flung itself out of the water trying to escape and it landed on the deck. I made a grab for it but I wasn't fast enough and it fell back into the sea. I'd been told that the fish in those waters were big but that tuna must have been two metres long.

My appetite for fish was awakened. I wanted a fish then no matter what size. The trawling line was ready with a strong hook, a wire trace and 250 kilo line. I tied it to the mast with a strong shock rubber and two minutes later got a bite. The fish was so strong that its pulling on the line made *Acrohc* lean over a fair bit while the shock rubber got thinner and thinner. I held the line to try to stop the rubber breaking thinking that sooner or later the fish had to tire. But I soon realised that something had to give and I didn't think it was going to be the fish. Suddenly the fish stopped playing around and just took off, breaking the rubber.

I had bean soup for dinner that night.

I wasn't going to give up though and the next day I prepared another line and added a safety line in case the new rubber broke; this time nothing would get away unless it really was a whale. But yesterday's big tuna was gone and there weren't any other fish around that day, except for the usual smallfry that were swimming in close formation beside *Acrohc*. Actually I recognised them as being the same ones that had joined me at the beginning of the leg. They were growing day by day and as they grew, I grew more tempted to get one for dinner.

For days I tried to get one of them on a small hook but they just ignored it. My speargun was too big for them. What I needed was something like a toy gun. I decided to make one and used whatever came to hand on board. I used the handle of the fish hook to make the base of the gun and easily found the rubber I needed. For the spear, I used the wire handle of my kerosene lamp with four straightened hooks on the end as a prong. I had some difficulty making the trigger but eventually found all I needed in the bits and pieces of my junk box.

After a few hours of fiddly work I ended up with a primitive looking sort of weapon that was ready to be put to the test. As usual my prey were swimming unsuspectingly close to the hull. I picked out a big one, fired and missed but at least the thing worked. I tried again and again, and finally ended up with two fish just big enough for a nice meal. I don't know what kind they were but they tasted nice. Next morning I caught more and pickled them.

Why should I fight with a ten foot tuna when I could choose from a selection of always handy fish? From then on I ate fish whenever I wanted and catching them was also a good way to pass the time.

The Satnav gave me the position again: 130 miles to go. We had been averaging 80 miles a day so I reckoned that the island should be visible the next day. I drank to that. And, indeed, the next day I sighted the island just before sunset. I had been told by François of *Mallamoc* that I would find a very beautiful bay to anchor in. In fact, La Baie Des Vierges is famous for being the most beautiful bay in the world. But we were still 20 miles away so I reduced sail so I could sleep that night and be fresh in the morning to sail around the island to the promised beautiful bay.

I knew there was no port of entry there and that I should call in first at Hiva-Oa for clearance but after 35 days of sailing I couldn't wait to see La Baie Des Vierges.

The island was beautiful and I didn't have to go ashore to find out how welcoming the people were. As I approached the bay an outrigger canoe met me and showed me a good anchorage. When later I took my first steps ashore and met some of the locals it became evident that anyone who approached them came away with a lot of fruit. And they weren't interested in selling it; money didn't seem to interest them. Often they were simply giving you a present or they would ask for something in exchange—things that usually weren't worth very much like a plastic raincoat, a ball of string or tools.

There weren't any large stores in the village, only a small shop that didn't stock very much other than some food—and it was never open. I must say I was disappointed I couldn't get a beer anywhere but I drank coconut milk instead. As a treat I ate fresh water shrimp which I found in the creeks that flowed in the tree covered valleys.

I had beautiful walks in the mountains that enclosed the village and the bay, discovering along the way that most of the island was lush and abundant with fruit. There was also wild game on the island and lots of fish around it. No wonder they weren't interested in money. Everything they needed was there. They didn't have television and they didn't bother listening to the world news on the radio.

Maybe for a few more years an outrigger will go out to meet an arriving yacht but one day what we call civilization will catch up with them. For the time being though it is still the most beautiful bay in the world.

The first evening I saw a square-rigger, all sails set, slowly entering the bay, looking just as it might have centuries ago. But this was no Spanish discoverer. It was a Norwegian ship on its way around the world. When I met the crew I learned that the *Svanhild* was a 100 year old ship that had been refitted by a large group of sailing enthusiasts. They were taking turns to crew her on the different legs of the planned three year tour. I thought it was a great idea and I believe there should be more people doing such projects.

We spent every evening on the *Svanhild* chatting about the people we'd met on our journeys. Often we found that we'd met the same people, for example, they'd also met Magnus and Dora the Icelanders. It was nice to be able to keep up with friends' movements via the 'coconut telegraph'. In fact each yacht knows of some other yachts and that way it is possible to keep track of some friends.

On my third day there I moved *Acrohc* alongside the *Svanhild* to take a picture of our two unusual boats together, then I joined them for a nice Norwegian style breakfast. After coffee it was time for me to leave; I had to declare my entry into the Marquesas before the authorities found me.

The "Svanhild" and her crew of 21

I was sorry to leave. The place had really put a spell on me and it wasn't a girl, or was it? Maybe it was the relaxed atmosphere of a tourist-free island.

*****

It took me two and a half days to reach Hiva-Oa which was only 45 miles away. The winds weren't good and I didn't want to use the motor as no cooling water was running through it. If it had been an old fashioned motor I could have fixed it before setting out but to even find the thermostat among the jungle of mechanical bits and tubes that made up this fancy motor was another thing.

Still, we reached the calm harbour late at night with a three foot tuna tied beside the cabin. I had caught it just before dark on approaching land. I intended to clean it in the morning but by then it was a bit on the smelly side and full of flies. I apologised to it and threw it over the side; at least the crabs could have a feed.

Atuana was a much bigger village. It had shops, a bar, a bank, a police station and a post office. My savings were spared by none of them—I was back in the real world. To start with, when you visit French Polynesia you have to deposit the equivalent of a return airfare to your country of origin. If not, they won't issue a visa and you have to stay away from all of the French Pacific islands, including Tahiti.

Henry came to the rescue once more and telexed a money order through to a bank in Tahiti for me. Within three days all was well. Of course that little transaction didn't come cheap. With transfer fee and loss of interest on the amount deposited I estimated that it cost each person applying for a visa $200.00. The *Svanhild* with her crew of 21 must have been a welcome sight to the local bank. She arrived a day later than me and we stayed for three days. It wasn't a bad place, almost the same as Fatu-Iva, but everything was too expensive . . . except the sandflies.

The only place I visited there was the last home of Paul Gauguin, the famous painter (he now stays at the cemetery). The rest of my time there was taken up with paperwork and catching up with the mail.

One morning *Svanhild* left to visit the north side of the island and later, after cleaning *Acrohc's* hull, I left. I had to be in Tahiti for Christmas as my younger brother Silvio was to meet me there for his holidays and I was anxious to see one of my family. With good winds I could make it easily with a stopover in the Tuamotus.

Off we went into the calm sea and more than ever I needed to catch up on some sleep; those short stopovers were killers for parties and late nights. But sleeping was out of the question on the first night. Rain squalls lasted all through the night and on the next day were still violent enough to claim another bucket from the deck.

The rest of the seven day trip was better but a bit hot and uncomfortable whenever I had to keep the hatch closed. There were some nice times on that trip with calm evenings when the dolphins stayed up late swimming through the plankton. I'd watch for hours then sleep well on those calm nights—this was rare but always a treat.

One morning Manihi came into view and a few hours later *Acrohc* sailed into the pass to tie on the dock behind *Blue Spurr*, an English yacht with a crew of four I'd met in Fatu-Iva. As I stepped ashore they told me what a great time they were having with the locals. Every night the islanders came to the dock and played the ukulele until the early hours of the morning, not just to charm the two girls on *Blue Spurr* but also because there wasn't much else to do.

Most of the islanders were involved in pearl farming in the sheltered waters of the big, shallow lagoon. Of all the low islands encircling the lagoon, only this one had a village. There were about a hundred people living in the village and I found them to be the friendliest people on earth! They, like most of the Polynesians I met, didn't find it so strange that I was sailing on a 12 foot boat, just a bit odd. Perhaps this was because they are the descendants of brilliant seafarers who sailed throughout the Pacific by means of astro-navigation, long before we even discovered the compass.

If the conditions for tying *Acrohc* had been better I would have stayed longer than two days, but there was a lot of current in the pass and the roughness made sleeping difficult.

The atoll of Ahe was within a day's sail. I was told it was a nicer place and there I could sail through the lagoon and tie at the dock near the village. The only trouble, apparently, could be getting through the pass at the right time—when the tidal current was favourable.

It was an easy sail there even though I'd made a mistake with tide times and had to motor against the strong current at the pass. But I wasn't the only one. *Blue Spurr* made the same mistake. From there on I used the motor when I needed it with or without cooling water. (In fact, I didn't fix it for the rest of my trip and to my surprise it didn't blow up.)

We sailed through the lagoon and instead of staying the planned two days, *Blue Spurr* and *Acrohc* stayed six.

I spent one day at a pearl farm where I learned a lot about the little 'balls'. There they grew the black ones. None were really black but the different colours were fascinating. The farmers collect the young mother-of-pearl, or nacre, by leaving a plastic mesh in the water for a month or so. Then they select the best ones and implant them with a pearl nucleus—a round piece of nacre. Then they put them back in the water, protected by wire cages. In about a year the mother-of-pearl has grown a protective layer over the foreign body which eventually becomes a pearl, hopefully smooth and perfectly round. That's when they become very valuable little 'balls'!

I also spent a day snorkelling with one of the yachties, exploring the reef inside the lagoon. An abundance of fish swam through the beautiful reefs providing plenty of food for the many sharks who consequently ignored us swimming around above them.

The atoll is a favourite of yachties not only for its beauty but also for a friendly Scottish-French couple who have lived there for many years. They have been accepted by the islanders and live a very simple life in a typical Polynesian hut with their two children. They were previously a yachting couple who had settled for the tranquil, natural life of the islands, believing it was the best place to raise a family. They act as an unofficial coconut telegraph office and are always happy to pass on information about other boats that have visited the atoll.

Ahe was also a place of little sleep but I wasn't complaining. The locals there also played the ukulele very well and if I stayed up late at night it was only because I was enjoying myself.

23-9 | meter 57 m. west, able to sail at 240°
POS 149 N. 84 22 W - Sleeping too good
lately, ice of Soil is coming off
but cloth is holding, log stoped again.
Soup of The day: bail
one cup of Sea Water + one of sweet W.
add 2 choped onions, one clove of carlic.
When boiling trown in a big Handful
of crushed noodles and a tin of
tomato paste with 2 spoons of o. oil
1 of Wastershire sauce and one tin of
creen peas, bon apetit, serves 4 or
one sailor. PS. needs Ventilation the next
day

24-9 | better sea - decided to check hull,
wile was falowing, not for long,
1/2 hour later cleaned Goose neck Bar-
lots of them, cleaned 3/4 - going a
lot faster.

~~/////~~
25 - | Good Going

26-9 - | Best day sum, 60 miles direct to
Gal. if it keeps should be there in 3 days

27 - | not as Good because of blow but
60 miles 270°

28 - | not Going south enough, litle wind
almost no Sun, Changed to large Scale
chart

29. | Some, almost calm, tried motor,
Was leaping, oil, put more, steel maxing
Hard sound but going real
thinking of motoring south, tried but
motor Went go, only 2 H., used main today

168

Chapter 11

Tahiti!

On the Sunday I said goodbye to the villagers and with *Blue Spurr* headed for the pass—this time with the right current!

At sea there was almost no wind but at least I could sleep. Once again I was soon left behind as *Blue Spurr* disappeared towards Tahiti. She was going via Rangiroa and I was sailing direct to Tahiti through the atolls. For the first two days the wind was light but then it changed to blow head on and *Acrohc* started wandering in every direction but the right one. I started getting a bit uptight as I realised more and more that I'd get to Tahiti later than I'd hoped. Normally this wouldn't have worried me but this time I wanted to be on time so I could spend Christmas with my brother. I also hoped to be able to refit *Acrohc* while I was there, so Tahiti wasn't just another port of call.

The leg was only 270 miles and the tradewinds were supposed to be reliable but it was still six days before I sighted Tahiti.

We entered the harbour just before night and I spotted *Dora*. Magnus threw me a line and I tied *Acrohc* to *Dora's* stern, then went on board to spend the evening catching up on their news. They'd sailed the same route as me but had called at different islands. They'd arrived a week earlier and were now waiting for a new autopilot to be sent out from Iceland—their old one had packed up during a storm.

(Like many other short-handed yachts Magnus and Dora didn't like the constant work of manually steering a boat.

That night they told me all about the place, where I would find the authorities, the fruit market, the post office, banks and the best chandler and sail repair shops. At every port there is always a yacht that's been there a few days and passes on information to a new arrival. This can save a lot of time.

Early the next day I went to the post office where news from home was waiting for me. Silvio was arriving on December 30th, just in time for the New Year's Eve party.

I sailed *Acrohc* to Maeva Beach, tying up in front of a big hotel where there was no traffic noise and no anchorage fees. I tied *Acrohc's* bow to a wall so that getting on and off would be easy as I had no proper dinghy. *Dora* and *Blue Spurr* joined me at Maeva Beach a couple of days later.

I had a beautiful Christmas dinner on *Dora*, then Silvio arrived. We had a happy reunion and I was so anxious for all the news from home that we sat up all night chatting.

The next day we rented a car not only to tour the island in but also for a place to sleep. *Acrohc* wasn't big enough for the two of us so we took it in turns to sleep in the car—the hotels there are only for millionaires.

Silvio was popular with the yachties and he also made friends with a few of the Tahitians. It is a pity though that Tahiti is one of the most expensive places on earth and this and the feuding between the French and the Polynesians left a bad taste.

The first sign of anti-French feeling was the attempted hijack in New Zealand of the plane Silvio was travelling on on his way to Tahiti. Then, as if this wasn't a fun enough experience, we found that because we spoke French the Tahitians thought we were French and this got us into trouble a few times. Much the wiser for the experience we stopped speaking French altogether while we were there. Maybe it wasn't the right place for a holiday after all! Silvio shortened his

170

stay to ten days and I stayed for only three weeks, just long enough to get the necessary jobs on *Acrohc* done.

Of course, Tahiti is a beautiful place but everything is extremely expensive and we felt quite poor there. Going to a restaurant, for example, was totally out of the question. The wages there are high and tax free. The government only taxes goods, so everything costs at least twice as much. This is okay for the Tahitians as their wages are also double but it's not so good for the tourists.

I bought just enough supplies for the trip to the Cook Islands, 600 miles away, and was happy to be off once more in search of greener and cheaper pastures. I was a bit worried about reaching my next port of call because, stupidly, I'd rested my bag containing my wallet and passport on the roof of our rented car while I did something and then, completely forgetting about it, we drove off. We went back to the spot as soon as I realised what I'd done but the bag was gone. There was no Australian Consul in Tahiti and the nearest one on my route was in Tonga. So, in the meantime, I just had to hope that the most that would happen to me would be that I was denied access to a port and not thrown in jail.

SILVER GULL

As when I'd left Darwin, it was cyclone season. The four I'd experienced previously should have taught me a lesson but by now I was convinced that *Acrohc* could take any kind of weather. Besides, not even cyclones could make me stay put in Tahiti—I just couldn't afford it.

So, sailing through the lagoon, I left Tahiti and again, to keep up the good habits, ran aground. But it wasn't serious and I pushed *Acrohc* into deeper water myself. Then we sailed through the pass and were back at sea again.

There wasn't much wind for the first few days but there were a lot of rain squalls. The trip should have taken eight to ten days but I was starting to doubt the existence of the tradewinds at all. The only wind we got was from squalls and it wasn't always favourable. It was upsetting to wake up and find that the windvane had faithfully followed the wind changes while I'd slept and we were going in totally the wrong direction.

I wished for a cyclone ... just a small one, but one that would bring some decent wind. The last one had passed through Samoa and then turned southeast, missing us by 350 miles. On the shortwave radio I learned that it made a big mess of Samoa, but I didn't get a single puff of wind from it.

I was getting bored again. Even the fish weren't biting. One day five dorados swam really close, but try as I might I just couldn't spear one. And *Acrohc* was sailing so slowly that even the sharks weren't interested in my trailing lure—one did have a taste of it but quickly spat it out in disgust.

It was only after ten days of light breezes that the wind slowly started to fill the sails. A big fish came up, his target a small fish that was accompanying us. I quickly threw the line out hoping for a sizeable catch. It took the lure straight away ... and kept it, breaking the trace wire. Ah well, I didn't want such a big fish anyway.

I replaced the trace wire and told it to find a smaller fish. It obeyed my orders for once and soon I was filleting a one foot bonito. By then it was quite late and I'd already had dinner but I still enjoyed eating some of the raw fish dipped in lemon sauce. The rest I preserved in jars. There were two ways of doing this. Either I boiled the fish in water and vinegar which preserved the fish for a few days, or I put the raw fish in a jar of water or vinegar and sealed it then boiled the whole thing. The latter way preserved the fish for much longer. Either way I always added lots of spices.

On the eleventh day a cargo ship passed only a few hundred metres from my stern, completely ignoring me. Then the wind started to get stronger and we passed the halfway mark that night, accompanied by lots of squalls. Fairly strong winds followed, pushing *Acrohc* along at three knots. We could have gone a little faster but the waves had become a bit nasty and were tossing us around badly.

The next day it was worse and I reduced canvas to just the staysail. I kept it that way for the rest of the trip not only because of the strong wind but I had also discovered a rip in the headsail's leech and small cuts along its foot. It was best not to use it at all or else the rips would spread and eventually ruin the whole sail. I would have to fix it at the next port but in the meantime the staysail would have to be enough.

Then, one evening, there were only 45 miles left to go before we'd reach Aitutaki, one of the Cook Islands. This was the perfect distance to arrive there the next morning. And, sure enough, as soon as the sun came out the next day I could see the island about ten miles away. The trip had taken 15 days, twice as long as it should have.

Aitutaki is an atoll group with one main island in the middle higher than the encircling ones. There was only one harbour and only one pass to enter the lagoon. We made it to the pass and *Acrohc's* size aroused the curiosity of a runabout returning from a diving trip. While they asked me questions, they led the way through the shallow pass to the dock. I tied up in the harbour and was soon chatting with the locals who speak both Maori and English, as the Cook Islands are closely associated with New Zealand.

I was relieved to find that no revolution was being planned here; everyone was friendly and helpful, if a bit unreliable. I'd seen this elsewhere in hot climates where 'in one hour' meant tomorrow and 'tomorrow' meant in a few days. This was probably the reason why the immigration man didn't show up. And when I went to see him the day after I arrived he seemed a little confused because I didn't have a passport. However, he seemed happy enough to use *Acrohc's* registration papers as identification.

I stayed there for six days, long enough to meet the locals, buy supplies and see the island dancers who performed for the few tourists on Friday nights. The Cook Islands also are Polynesian but the islanders' dances are different from the Tahitians—they are much livelier.

I also met Father George, the resident Catholic priest. In his slightly Dutch accent, he invited me to his home where he proudly showed me his collection of filled visitors books. In 40 years he'd collected thousands of signatures and it seemed that there was a story attached to each of them. I had the honour of being the first entry in the eighth volume. Books like these provide a good reference source for checking up on the whereabouts of cruising friends. It's a shame that there isn't someone with such a hobby in every port. There are others but Father George keeps the best set of visitors books I've ever seen.

He talked a lot about the nine foot yacht *Winds Will* which held the record for the smallest boat to have crossed the Atlantic. Her American skipper, Bill Dunlop, had been attempting to set a record for the Pacific as well, but after he left Aitutaki (two years earlier than my visit) he was never seen again. I had heard a lot about him and his boat and felt that we would have had a lot in common. Pity I never met him!

Father George had no doubt that I would succeed. He thought that *Acrohc* was a safe boat and he believed that I had taken every precaution in preparing her. I hoped he was right. The following Monday I was ready to leave and walked down to the immigration office for clearance. I found the immigration officer in his office but he told me that it was his day off and that I would have to wait until the following day when he would be back on duty. I thought that if he wasn't prepared to do a mere five minutes work for me, I wasn't prepared to wait another day so I left without clearance.

At 3.00pm I untied the lines, motored out and ran aground in the pass, but I was soon back out at sea with the old feeling that once again I hadn't stayed long enough ashore. I was leaving a beautiful Pacific island with a lagoon full of fish and good spots for diving. I hadn't even had the chance to get to know the nice island girls. Yes, there was no doubt that I should have stayed longer than six days but there was also no denying that I was in a hurry to get home. It was sad that I was using some of the most beautiful places on earth as mere stepping stones. Tonga, 900 miles away, was my next stepping stone.

* * * * *

As always I looked forward to good winds. On the first day there was barely any wind and on the second and third day gale force winds brought nasty waves that crashed over *Acrohc*. Probably because I was getting used to rough weather I didn't mind so much. But a particularly vicious wave swept over the deck and tore through the staysail. My trusty staysail that had until then resisted everything that had been thrown at it was ripped badly at the bottom. If I wanted to save it from being completely wrecked I'd have to bring it down for repairs quickly. It wasn't a safe thing to do in that weather but I had no choice. A torn and flapping sail wouldn't last long in that sort of wind. Besides, I'd get a wash while I was out there.

I got the sail down with a lot of difficulty and tied it down securely. The headsail would just have to do for the moment. This wasn't the first storm it'd had to cope with anyway.

The next day Australia lost the Americas Cup and we were becalmed! I also found out that if I wanted the Satnav to keep working I'd have to get a new battery. My old faithful battery just wouldn't keep charged for very long. At first I suspected a fault in the wiring but then I found that one of the elements had gone. I'd just have to nurse it until we reached the next port. I'd got used to the Satnav and I didn't feel like having to mess around with the sextant again. Unlike the sailing 'purists', I am a firm believer that a sextant should be kept on board for decorative purposes only and perhaps as a back up. Undoubtedly it is an instrument with a lot of merit and I agree that its use should still be taught in the sailing schools, but it is a bit out of place in the computer age. This brings me back to my theory of how easily we become 'soft'; you see, first it's a calendar then it's a Satnav . . !

For the next 16 days we had every kind of weather. The most annoying types were the squalls, the complete absence of wind, or the headwinds. This was cyclone season weather. With a bit of luck we could escape the actual cyclones but there was no escaping the frequent squalls. In the cyclone season the usually reliable tradewinds become confused and there are long periods of calm. It is also humid and terribly hot.

During the calm periods I ran the motor to charge the battery so that I could keep using the Satnav.

BROWN BOOBY

By the seventeenth day, another rough day, I was nearing Tongatapu and I had to stay up all night because I didn't have the large-scale chart for that area. My best chart only showed the contours of the island roughly so I had to keep a look out for the harbour lights and especially for reefs. I'd looked for a better chart for Tongatapu in Tahiti but the only one I could get was a hand drawn chart from *Dora*. It looked more like a pirate's treasure map than a chart. It was nice but it didn't help me with navigation at all!

The next morning I was within sight of land but we'd gone a bit far and I had to tack back against a strong wind. I decided to take a short cut which I never would have done if I'd had the proper charts as it took us through a maze of reefs that became shallower and shallower until *Acrohc* bumped onto the coral. At one stage the water under us was only two feet deep but it was too late to turn back by then so I pulled hard on the sails to make us lean over enough to raise the keel and release us from each of the little reefs we got stuck on.

The outboard surpassed itself. Not only was there no cooling water but the oil light also went off. And half the time the propeller was out of the water and at quite an angle. Still, although the manual said 'Do not store sideways,' it didn't say anything about not running it sideways!

When we'd finally got ourselves out of that mess I threw out the anchor just offshore from a resort on the small Atata Island and had a rest; after all, there's only so much a man can take. It wasn't too far to the shore so I decided to swim over for a beer before I headed off to the harbour, still nearly five miles away across the bay.

I stayed a bit too long because it was low tide when I finally got back to *Acrohc* and she was leaning over at 45 degrees. I decided it didn't matter. The high tide was due around midnight and then I could move a bit further out. I'd sail to town in the morning.

My plan would have worked but in the dark we kept bumping into coral, no matter which way we went and I just couldn't find any deep water. I got sick of trying and decided to spend the night aground. As the tide dropped *Acrohc* slowly leaned over. By six o'clock in the morning she was completely over on her side in only 20 centimetres of water and we were totally surrounded by coral. I joined all the lines I had and tied an anchor to one end. Then I walked with the anchor to the edge of the reef, dropped it and waited for the tide to come up. While I waited I busied myself with disinfecting all the cuts on my feet and legs I'd got from walking on the coral.

When the water was about three feet deep I started pulling on the line from the mast to make *Acrohc* lean sideways. This way, and with a bit of help from the strong wind, I inched her over the reef. By noon we were anchored in six metre deep water. It was a bit late to set out for the harbour and there was still a strong wind that would be against us so I got down to cleaning up the mess inside caused by the groundings.

My work was interrupted by a visit from the people of the resort. They persuaded me to go back to the resort with them for a few drinks and said they'd deliver me back to *Acrohc* later that night. I just couldn't refuse such an offer.

The next day I motored to town, successfully avoiding a few large patches of coral on the way. By ten o'clock I finally reached the small harbour of Nuku'Alofa. It was a bit crowded as the bad weather had kept all of the fishing boats at home but I managed to squeeze *Acrohc* in and tied up to a big yacht. I looked up at the dock and saw Melissa, the girl I'd met in Cape Town, waiting for me. We hadn't meant what we'd had in Cape Town to go on but we'd kept in touch. When I was in South Africa she told me she wanted to leave the country for various reasons.

After visiting Australia she decided to make it her new home. I knew we'd meet there so I decided it was a good reason to stop for a bit longer than usual and get some proper rest for a change.

But, first I had to get clearance. I didn't have a passport and I also had no exit clearance from my last port and no crew list; nothing, in fact, except *Acrohc's* registration papers. I was a most unusual case but the Tongan authorities were patient and, as I got a new passport from the local Australian High Commission the same day (which made me almost legal), they chose to ignore the other missing paper.

Melissa and I found ourselves a comfortable guesthouse which was reasonably priced and there I started to relax after the events of that last leg. I would have preferred to stay on *Acrohc* though as, although it was a safe harbour, I didn't like to stay away from her too long. Mind you, we visited her everyday.

According to Melissa everything I owned needed washing! I suppose my things did smell from being damp all the time but I'd got used to it. Melissa also gave the inside of *Acrohc's* cabin a good scrubbing and I had to admit that it looked much better for it. So, the first chores completed, we started sightseeing.

Tongatapu is the main island of the Tongan Kingdom. However, it is still a small island and the tourist tour didn't take long. Within a few days we'd seen the blow-holes, the remains of royal tombs and the 'royal bats'—so named because only the royal family can hunt them. We also visited an ancient monument called the Trilithon, two 40 ton coral rocks planted upright with a lintel joining them. I was told that the small carving on the lintel was a seasonal calendar. The whole structure was once the gateway of a royal palace which no longer exists. Another feature of Tonga is the local handicrafts which are popular with the tourists.

As in most of Polynesia they make a bark cloth, called by the Tongans, 'tapa'. They take the bark of a certain tree, soak it in sea water, beat it until it is very thin and then decorate it with paints which

The Royal Gate or a calendar?

are also made the traditional way from plants. I tried my hand at beating the bark with the wooden mallets they use but was laughed at—apparently it's a job exclusively for women!

Basket weaving is also popular as are wood and black coral carving. I was pleased to meet the brothers and cousins of Tonga Bill, the fellow who had done the carving on *Acrohc's* bowsprit. His relatives were also good carvers but I still thought that Tonga Bill was the best. It was a shame that he wasn't in Tonga when we were there. I was told that he'd married Christine, the French girl at Reunion. Apparently they were still cruising around, at that time in New Zealand, and were expected in Tonga in a few months time.

Melissa and I also took *Acrohc* for a sail to a nearby island on Sunday. By the way, Sundays in Tonga are reserved for going to church. Anyone found working, dancing or doing anything else for that matter, does so at the risk of being fined. The tourists are tolerated but not wearing a shirt in the street is fineable and an unforgivable sin.

The king rules the islands in a most traditional way. If it weren't for modern things like cars and telephones it would feel as though you were back in the Middle Ages complete with royals, nobles and commoners.

Another strange thing about Tongans is that they can be too friendly and willing to please. This is not always a good thing because they might answer you with a yes or a no depending on what they believe will please you. And even more confusing is the way they say 'Yes'—instead of nodding their heads they raise their eyebrows.

I still don't know how they say 'No' but I do know it's not by shaking their heads because one day I asked a lady for water to fill *Acrohc's* freshwater tank by pointing questioningly to the big rainwater tank and then to the jerrycans I was carrying. She shook her head vigorously as if to say no, so I said thanks all the same and turned to go. But she called me back and pointed to the big tank and I understood that I could help myself. I had to make three trips and it was the same story each time. Some time later it struck me that she wasn't saying 'no' to me at all and I had a good laugh thinking that it wasn't any wonder that they think all 'palangis' (foreigners) are crazy.

At least I must be crazy because when a television production crew from Brisbane turned up at Tonga to film *Acrohc* I had the bright idea of sailing to Atata Island, the one with all the coral reefs where I'd first landed (literally). The crew wanted to get some shots of *Acrohc* sailing into a lovely sunset and sunrise, they also wanted to film a night performance of Tongan dances that was to be held at the resort.

The sunset was spoiled by clouds and I ended up on the coral again (although not badly stuck). The dances were worth seeing though and among the dancers I recognised the barmaid, the cook, the gardeners, in fact, most of the resort employees, and some of the local fishermen. They performed the real traditional dances and it was easy to see that they enjoyed performing as much as we enjoyed watching. It was a good night but the sunrise was also a failure because a squall got in the way. So much for getting up at 4:30am!

Although Tongans were once a fierce race of warriors, Tonga was named the Friendly Islands by Captain Cook because of the great welcome he got when he arrived and because he didn't know about their plan to burn his ship for its metal (so precious to the Pacific islanders). He left before the event, spoiling their plans. So, the 'Friendly Islands' remained the 'Friendly Islands' and the warriors missed out on their raid. They don't burn ships anymore and the name really suits them. . .after all, they only wanted some nails!

Tonga is situated just on the edge of the International Dateline, where Sunday becomes Monday. It is said that 'Tonga is where time begins' but, to me, it just continued.

Chapter 12

GOING HOME

Acrohc had a new battery, mended sails, a clean cabin and she had been well scrubbed below the waterline. She also had a full watertank and well stocked lockers. I'd had a good rest and was ready to be on my way to the big welcome home ceremony scheduled to be held in Brisbane on the 16th of May by the City of Brisbane. The organisers of the event had agreed on that day so I could catch the tidal current in the river at 6:15 in the morning and reach the spot where *Acrohc* had been launched by 2:00pm. The Lord Mayor would welcome me then *Acrohc* would be put on display. It just happened to be 'The Year of the River' in Brisbane so the Council wanted to make the most of the event. In fact, I had been asked to keep a low profile until we were actually in the river and to avoid the media until I arrived in the city itself.

I had my doubts about being able to go along with their plans for although *Acrohc* often went under water, she certainly wasn't a submarine and I was sure that we'd be spotted when we arrived in Moreton Bay. There are usually a lot of fishing boats in the bay and someone was bound to contact the media after sighting *Acrohc*. But, who was I to argue so I went along with their plans.

It is not easy for a sailing boat to arrive anywhere on a set date. However, the idea was a 20 day sail to Norfolk Island, two weeks rest there then a two week sail to Moreton Bay. I chose the Norfolk Island route, further south, instead of going via Noumea. It was 100 miles longer but it was to reduce the chances of meeting a cyclone. Also, New Caledonia's prices rival Tahiti's! It was a shame. Noumea has a lot to offer including a near revolution, but never mind.

Norfolk Island has no proper harbour and I expected problems landing there, but I had been told that the island was very beautiful and didn't have a lot of coral which was reason enough for going there!

It was the 24th of March and *Acrohc* and I had to get going. I would see Melissa in Brisbane.

It started raining just as I got underway and the wind was starting to blow very hard from the east. We had to try to get out of the bay preferably without disturbing too many polyps' homes. But with the help of the sounder and the 'Saint Who Looks After Dumb Sailors', I found the channel and made it through the gap in the reef and into the open sea without mishap. It was 1,100 miles to Norfolk Island, a maximum of four weeks based on previous performances.

I was expecting to be seasick after a month ashore but despite the rough weather I was alright. I killed seven cockroaches that had obviously left their rough quarters on Tongan fishing boats in favour of a cosy bed on *Acrohc* and later killed three more. That was the only time I had cockroaches on board and I did my best to get rid of them. There was no room for stowaways on this trip!

On the first two days we had strong following winds and rain. Then the wind turned and came from the south and the sun shone. The cabin became very hot as I couldn't open the hatch. But I expected the conditions to improve as we travelled towards the south.

On the sixth day, we passed half the world—I mean longitude 180 degrees—and started sailing on the eastern side of the globe. The chart now went from 180 degrees down and as Brisbane is at 153 degrees, the countdown started.

We travelled 90 miles on both the fifth and sixth days but I was still stuck inside; I couldn't open the hatch and sit outside to pass the time. I even had to put curtains up at the portholes to stop the sun heating up the cabin too much. This, of course, also stopped the view but luckily I am not claustrophobic.

Cooking was difficult due to *Acrohc's* wild motion and the occasional wave crashing down on her, but I didn't mind too much as, if our speed was good, I felt good and each day we were one or two degrees closer to home. (One degree equals 60 nautical miles).

On the seventh and eighth days we did even better covering almost 100 miles each day.

On the ninth day it was a bit calmer and the wind turned to blow on our starboard side. Finally I could open the hatch. Our speed was still fairly good because with less wind I could unfurl the headsail completely and the waves weren't affecting *Acrohc's* course. I preferred these conditions even at the expense of ten or 20 miles a day—at least I could cook properly.

Days ten and 11 were a bit disappointing as, with all sorts of winds, we only covered 50 miles each day. On slow days like those I started thinking about my three years of sailing and the things I'd done wrong. For example, it would have been more comfortable in strong winds with a shorter mast; my mistake had been to believe that I'd find mostly light winds. Another mistake was that I hadn't installed a built-in fuel tank in the bow so I had to keep the fuel on deck.

Most yachtsmen envied my chart table because it was big but I felt that it was too big. If it had been 30 centimetres shorter it would have been easier to slide and open. The bunk should also have been smaller so that in rough weather it was easier to hold on. But I didn't really mind its size; two persons had to sleep there on many occasions!

The ventilation too could have been better. Instead of just one dorado vent I should have installed four. I am sure I could have found room. And the stove was too dangerous. Perhaps gas would have been safer to operate in rough weather. The fire on the way to Madagascar was entirely my fault but the near repeat of the incident on the way to Galapagos was due to a faulty burner. Maybe there is no safe way to cook!

I didn't think that I could have improved much on the hull shape, rudder and keel—but perhaps I could have had less draft with a shorter mast. However the sail handling system was great and so was the self-steering.

Another mistake was that I should have had a Satnav from the very beginning. My running aground at Cape Town was sheer stupidity. Sure there was the 'Black South Easter' but when I realised that I couldn't make it to the harbour I should have sailed towards the open sea where it was safer. It may have been very rough out there but there wouldn't have been any rocks or beaches to run into.

As for the problems I'd had with my skin on the way to the Cocos Islands, well, it was just bad luck that I'd had to sail through four cyclones. Skin problems aside, I'd sail through cyclone seasons again as long as I knew the boat was strong.

The minor groundings all over the world were clearly my fault. There was no excuse for it but maybe knowing that *Acrohc* would be none the worse for small bumps and scrapes made me careless. It could have been avoided in Tonga if I hadn't tried taking a short cut, or maybe just having a proper chart would have prevented it. When I couldn't buy a proper chart, I should have asked my brothers to send me one.

There were countless other mistakes and I am sure that I will make just as many more in the future. Maybe the whole trip had been a mistake—on more than one occasion I'd wished that I'd never started it or that I'd built a large boat which would have taken me around the world in comfort. But no matter how strong and well thought out a boat is, there are risks that can't be avoided when sailing single handed, like not being able to keep a constant watch for ships or even whales for that matter.

But despite it all I never gave up the idea of doing another out of the ordinary trip but not in *Acrohc*—she'd done her job.

I'd gained a lot in those three years, not material things but things like experiences at sea that only a yachtsman can have, and many friendships . . . I'd met a lot of people simply because I had a 'funny' boat.

How else could I have fulfilled my ambition to write a book? The trip made that possible too. And who knows, one day I might have grandchildren—I would tell them about the different people I'd met, the languages they spoke, the way they lived and their customs. I could tell stories of strange animals, great forests and volcanos. Of course, I may never have grandchildren and spoiled brats may not be interested in listening to my boring old stories . . . but at least I will have something to remember in my old age.

I had also learned a lot about life at sea and I had discovered how much I could endure. The trip hadn't changed my views on life itself, nor had it changed me as a person. I know a bit more but maybe just because I am older and I've seen different things. Perhaps my values had changed . . . maybe it had been worth it.

I had a lot of these sort of reflections on slow days as we sailed towards Norfolk.

The twelfth day out coincided with Mum's birthday. We were going slowly and it was cloudy—235 miles to go. The next day it became a bit too windy. The sails suffered from the wind that night and were ripped in two places. They still held the wind well though.

On the sixteenth day I couldn't believe the wind. I was only 60 miles from land and it was as though someone had 'pulled the plug'. I pictured a man saying, 'Right! That's it! You've had your share.' But we only had 24 hours of calm before it started blowing again, this time from the north. I reduced sail to slow down for the night and managed to be near the south of Norfolk Island by early morning. This was supposed to be my last port of call and a two week stopover before home and it looked very nice too.

Before entering Sydney Bay, I contacted the shore authorities and was told to anchor between the jetty and the cargo ship *Ile De*

Lumiere. The ship was going to be unloading all day so I was able to use the ferrying boats to get ashore. It was too far and too rough to have used my dinghy so I was lucky that the ship happened to be there. No boats are kept in the water there at any other time because it is too exposed. The lighters (boats used to ferry the cargo) are unloaded at the big concrete jetty by a mobile crane. As soon as the work is done, everything, including the crane, is removed from the dock.

The lighters of Norfolk Island. They are used to unload cargo in the exposed harbour. They can handle anything up to a bus.

When I anchored, Customs came on board and we completed the initial paperwork. Then I was taken ashore where I found that *Acrohc* was a star and everyone was ready to help. I was driven to the Governor for approval to store *Acrohc* on land, then to Customs and Immigration. I was given a quick medical and free accommodation was arranged for me as I wasn't going to be allowed to stay on *Acrohc* once she was dry stored.

By 3.00pm all was ready. At five o'clock they would tow *Acrohc* to the jetty and the crane would lift her out of the water and onto a truck. She'd then be unloaded in the harbour's car park. There were no problems in sight except maybe the swell at the jetty where they would be lifting her out. I didn't really like the idea of *Acrohc* being left in a car park but after all, the accommodation was free and the owner a nice guy. The island also had many things of interest and everyone made me welcome . . .

I still had one tiny worry gnawing at me. That harbour could only be used when the wind was from the north. When the wind blew from the south it built up swells good enough for a surfing championship to be held and *Acrohc* could be stuck on the island when the time came to leave.

I did a quick mental appraisal of the pros and cons and decided to leave, making an extra stop on the way to Brisbane at Lord Howe Island. I had to act fast as the lighters stopped work at 5.00pm and were taken out of the water and I didn't want to be stuck ashore.

I cleared with Customs in a hurry so that I could leave the next day. I checked for mail, rang home and then went to the local newspaper's office where I was expected. After a warm reception and a couple of pictures for the next edition, I had a quick shower. Then the editor drove me back to the jetty. It was five o'clock by that stage and I was just in time to get a lift in one of the lighters back to *Acrohc*.

I had intended to go ashore again next morning to do some shopping and, if I had time, accept the Captain's offer to visit *Ile De Lumiere*. But in the meantime I anchored a bit further out where there was less swell and slept until midnight when the wind started turning and the rocking got too much for comfort. The anchor line was taking a lot of strain and although I didn't like having to move anchor in the middle of the night, it had to be done. I moved further out but still had to keep watch until morning as the sea was still too rough for my liking.

When morning came the swell was still building up, beginning to break into rollers as it passed us. *Acrohc* was being lifted a good five metres by each wave. I switched the VHF on and heard that the *Ile De Lumiere* was going to move to the north of the island to complete her unloading. I realised that I would have to do the same if I wanted to get a lift ashore. I also realised that if I didn't get out of there myself, and fast, I'd be in trouble as the waves were starting to break even closer, threatening to capsize *Acrohc*.

But there was a problem. The bottom was all rocks and the anchor chain had got tangled. It was holding *Acrohc's* bow under water every time a swell lifted her; on several occasions half of the deck was completely under water. There was no way I could retrieve the anchor by diving for it; the water there was too deep and the swell too strong. I tried lengthening the line and motoring in every direction hoping that this would untangle the chain but I had to give up when the waves started breaking just about where I was. There was nothing else for it but to cut the line and get the hell out of there as fast as possible. If not I'd join the two other yachts that had broken their anchor lines less than a month earlier and were completely wrecked on the rocks.

Now I was left with only one anchor with no chain, only rope. To try to re-anchor with that would be suicide as the rocks would easily cut through the rope and we'd be swept onto the rocky coastline in no time at all. Well, I didn't really need to mail my postcards, or buy fruit and veggies, or make that last phone call and I could do without fresh bread and margarine which were really only luxury items; what I did need was to be out in the open sea with room to breathe. I wanted to let the shore know what was happening but my VHF didn't have an outside aerial and by then I couldn't open the hatch so it was impossible.

So, within what seemed to be a very short period of time, *Acrohc* was back at sea. It was just like the previous day; same wind, same direction, same heeling. With a feeling of disbelief I rolled a blanket beside the seat to make a flat surface to sit on, pushed a cushion behind me and looked at the waves through the porthole; just like the days before. It was as though my stop there had been a dream. Had I really spent a day running around on that island? I must have. I had four unmailed postcards, complete with stamps and, yes, I had taken a few snapshots of the magnificent pine trees. Behind me, through the porthole, I could still see them.

The well grassed hills had looked so nice and the people had been so warm and friendly. They had told me they 'talked funny' because most of them were descendants of the Bounty mutineers and their Tahitian wives. (And maybe that's why the girls are so beautiful.) Although the original settlers moved to Norfolk from Pitcairn Island in 1856, their descendants have kept their unique language, a mixture of old English and Tahitian.

Norfolk Island is now an Australian Territory. It is duty free so it attracts an enormous number of tourists. It is also an island of spectacular, natural beauty and it was a great shame that my stay had been so short. I hadn't expected so many difficulties in anchoring there or getting ashore; I didn't believe that it could be more difficult than at St. Helena. I had also intended to repair the sails at Norfolk Island but that would just have to wait now.

Never mind. Ahead lay Lord Howe Island which had a nice lagoon to anchor in. It too was supposed to be beautiful and it wasn't too far out of my way. So the sailing went on. We had about 500 miles to go.

The first night was rough as I was beating close to the wind. In the morning I found that the staysail was torn beyond repair. I didn't have a chance to bring it in during that entire trip because of the weather. A few rips had also appeared in the headsail but it seemed to be holding okay.

On the fourth day there were still lots of big waves coming at us from every direction. I was locked securely inside *Acrohc* so I wasn't worried even when the waves broke over the top of the cabin. Chopping onions in the confined space proved to be hazardous and I ended up in tears! I was comforted by the Satnav which said that Lord Howe was only 330 miles away.

During that leg I thought a lot about the end of my voyage. To also pass the time I often had a snacks or hot drinks and I went back to my routine of having a hot meal in the evening and sleeping at night. On dark nights when the waves broke over the cabin it was fun watching the luminous plankton sliding down the perspex outside the portholes and I often fell asleep marvelling at those 'fireflies of the sea'.

Life was beautiful no matter what the weather brought; there were only 1,000 miles to go and then I'd be home. In fact, my morale was so high that I could even ignore a nasty rash on my bottom. It had begun long before, soon after I'd left the Cook Islands, as two or three lumps rather like mosquito bites. I had intended to get it checked out at Norfolk but, obviously, hadn't had time. However, soon after I left Norfolk it started spreading and became extremely itchy. I took some anti-rash pills but soon had twice as many spots and sitting became uncomfortable. Finally the spots turned into sores so I decided to take antibiotics but by then the itchy lumps had spread to my legs and back and even my arms. I was beginning to worry as the nearest doctor was a week away but I couldn't do anything more about it; the sailing had to go on.

The fifth day brought even bigger and more confused waves. I had been told that these were normal conditions in the Tasman Sea.

It was still too rough on the sixth day to venture out and recover the torn staysail but we only had 185 miles left to go and I was pleased with the 75 miles a day we were managing with the genoa still holding. If it weren't for the crazy waves we'd have been doing a lot more. By day seven there were only 84 miles to go. We'd done 101 miles in 24 hours.

The night had been windy and rough but the good going boosted my morale even more and helped me not to think about the fast spreading, itchy and by then painful rash. It looked as though we'd get to Lord Howe the next day in daylight and this made me very happy.

On the morning of the eighth day I got an early fix from the magic box and found that we only had 32 miles to go. I was still sure that we'd arrive in daylight. I had been worried about arriving at night as I had no chart of the island. I knew its position from reference books and a general map of the Pacific Islands, but that map didn't show water depth and there was always the possibility that there were a few rocks offshore that weren't illustrated.

This time I wasn't guilty of not having a chart, it was simply that I hadn't intended going to Lord Howe. Of course, it could be argued that a prudent sailor would be carrying the chart just in case but, at $12.00 a chart, who could afford to be prudent? (And even being economical I used more than 70 charts on the whole trip.)

Anyway, as predicted, I sighted the island before noon. The waves were increasing as we got nearer to the island and consequently our speed dropped, but I thought we could still make it. I went on believing this until it started to get dark and by the time I reached the southern most point of the island it was completely dark. The unreliable depth-sounder had to be my eyes from then until we reached the lagoon entrance on the other side. Then I would call up the authorities and they could tell me where to find the pass.

When we rounded the southern end of the island we met those notorious wind gusts that are created by mountains. Luckily I was ready for them and I kept the headsail very reduced but the torn staysail which was still out disappeared piece by piece. For about a half an hour the blustery winds blew from every direction at intervals of five minutes, then we got out of their reach and started sailing again, the motor having given up. (I thought it was out of fuel but it turned out later to be water in the carburettor.)

It was still very windy but the waves were more manageable now that we were on the western side of the island. As I approached the lagoon I got on the radio and called, 'Lord Howe, Lord Howe. Yacht *Acrohc*, yacht *Acrohc*, come in please.'

Soon the reply came, 'Calling yacht, this is Lord Howe.'

Gale force winds ripped the stay sail. It was first ripped by a wave and the wind finished it off.

After the usual information was passed between us I asked for advice. 'Can you inform me what is best to do? I've lost my good anchor and I am out of fuel.'

'It's not possible to enter the lagoon at night. You must anchor outside until morning. What anchor gear have you left?' they replied.

'A fisherman anchor, no chain but lots of 12 millimetre rope.'

'That rope will never be strong enough,' came back the confident reply.

'I should point out that it is only a 12 foot yacht,' I said.

'Could you repeat?'

I obliged, '12 feet; three and a half metres.'

'Well, shiver me timbers! Just wait there, we are coming out to give you a tow.'

The voice turned out to belong to Clive Wilson, the Port Captain, and it was he and his son who eventually came out in a launch to bring us in. They were taking a bit of a risk going through the passage in the dark to 'rescue' me and I felt a bit guilty. It wasn't an emergency; I could have tried anchoring where I was or I could have simply sailed around until daylight. Still, I preferred the idea of being safely inside the lagoon so I went along with it.

While they were towing me in Clive radioed ahead to Customs. He told them that I'd had a bad time and that I couldn't wait until morning to come ashore as I needed a shower and a good rest. I was listening in on the conversation and when I heard the word 'shower' I reacted to it like a five year old who's been told that Santa Claus is coming.

We moored *Acrohc* and went ashore to meet Tom, the Customs man. He drove me to his office to do some paperwork and he contacted a doctor to make a morning appointment. Then Tom drove me to Clive's home for the shower.

For some reason I was finding it more difficult to walk straight than usual. I was reeling around like a drunk, only just managing to stay upright. But I had a lovely, long, hot shower and soon felt human again. Then Clive showed me where I could sleep and said, 'Good night, see you in the morning for breakfast.' He also told me that the treatment I was getting wasn't given to every yachtsman and that they never usually go through the pass at night as it is full of coral heads. Also, they had only just got back into bed after rescuing a catamaran that had slipped its anchor and landed on the reef! I felt even more guilty then but he brushed my apologies aside saying, 'With you it's different, it wasn't your fault. Anyone can have a spell of bad luck and lose an anchor. It's people that do the wrong thing and then call for help that I get mad with.'

*****

I hadn't expected to be able to sleep well that night as the sudden change would not be easy to adjust to and my sores were still extremely itchy. In fact, I woke up often to have a good scratch but many times I woke up because I was reaching for the compass light. Then I'd slowly realise that the bed wasn't moving and it was softer. So I'd tell myself that there's nothing to check, you can go back to sleep.

As for my itch, it turned out to be a harmless bug infection that had been aggravated by the salt sores. 'Staph', apparently, is a common bug often found in hospitals. Many people are carriers but it's usually harmless unless it finds a wound to live in. The doctor concluded that my sitting for prolonged periods in the damp had provided the perfect environment for it to thrive. It is curable though and all I needed was a heavy dose of antibiotics for a couple of weeks. He also said my diet at sea was perfectly adequate and had nothing to do with it.

So, all was well, but what does a seaman do when he gets into port? He usually goes looking for girls and gets drunk. However, I want to point out that I am not always guilty of that sort of behaviour . . . well, I don't always get drunk . . . but this time I had to keep away from alcohol because of the antibiotics and away from the girls because the rash was contagious (besides, it was pretty awful to look at as well as itchy).

To take my mind off that, I kept myself busy with the usual chores. One job was to wash out all my clothes; some were completely ruined from being permanently wet from the condensation in the cabin. Another job was to find something suitable to make a solid floor for the dinghy that I'd got in Panama, so it wouldn't fold up around me when I stepped into it.

The guys from the local council kindly supplied me with a suitable floor for the dinghy and they also supplied me with the procedure for Friday nights on the island: dinner at a guesthouse, on to the dance at the Bowls Club, from there to a party on Ned's Beach and at daylight home, to recover.

I went as far as the dance but one of the problems was refusing the offers for drinks. And, for the first time in my life, I had to discourage the advances of a pretty girl! There was just no point trying to go on under those appalling conditions. (The second Friday wasn't much better. The rash was under control but still hadn't completely cleared up.)

One day the editor of the local newspaper suggested that I move *Acrohc* to the jetty to give the locals a chance to get a closer look at her and I was happy to do so during the next high tide. There were big crowds at the jetty that afternoon and *Acrohc* was very popular. One of the onlookers turned out to be the local schoolmaster. He invited me to chat to the children, just as I had done in Cocos, only this time the children were all together in the activity room so it didn't take all day.

After a few hours of answering the enthusiastic questions of the children, I agreed to take *Acrohc* back to the jetty on the following Tuesday, the day of my departure, so the class could look at her.

In the three weeks I spent on Lord Howe I met most of the 250 residents. I was also shown how they climb the Lord Howe palm trees for seeding. Four species of palm tree are native to the island and these species are exported to all over the world. To climb them they place a circular strap around their feet and 'hop' up, clamping their feet around the trunk at each hop. To climb down they release the pressure on the belt and slide quickly down the smooth trunk. It's a very efficient way to climb trees—a lot faster than the way I climb coconut trees, the Pacific islanders way, which is walking up the trunk.

The main form of transport on the island is bicycles but I had to walk because of my sore bottom. I still saw a lot of the island though and it proved to be well worth the effort.

Tuesday came and this time *Acrohc* attracted an even bigger crowd. First the children came on board in groups of four and each had a turn sitting inside the cabin. I'd got used to the smell of the cabin but on humid days even I found the atmosphere in there a bit overpowering so it was a tribute to the politeness of the children that only a few remarked on it. Then the adults turned up in force and, as the event had been publicised in the local paper, I am sure that just about everyone on the island, including the tourists, packed onto the jetty.

Throughout the voyage I had been carrying a spinnaker that had been recut as a genoa for a spare sail. The other genoa was irreparable so when I left the jetty for the final leg of the trip I unfurled it for the first time. I didn't like its shape but its bright red and blue colours looked beautiful.

Acrohc had to be in Brisbane by the 16th. We had only 400 miles to go and 11 days to do it. I decided that if we were a bit early we'd just have to spend a few days in Moreton Bay as I had no intention of aimlessly sailing up and down the coast waiting for the right date. I expected the winds to be good all the way but I was a little worried about the northerly current near the mainland so I allowed a few extra days in case it interfered with the timing.

*****

There were a lot of people waving from the quay when I left Lord Howe and two launches escorted *Acrohc* through the pass.

I was really on the last leg home and soon I'd be no longer living on *Acrohc* as I had done for almost three years. I couldn't decide if I was happy or sad about it but I was definitely looking forward to throwing that yellow smoke flare when I reached the mouth of the Brisbane River.

On the third day out I saw a ship. At first sighting it didn't appear to be moving towards us but it was and eventually missed us by only 50 metres. It was a very close shave and it would have been funny to be run over after three years at sea, when only three days from home. After that I kept a good look out as I knew we'd meet more ships on nearing the coast.

On the next night we were caught in a storm that lasted all through the following day too. For only the second time in the trip I believed that *Acrohc* was going to capsize when a wave that thought it was smarter than the others hit us, but all it succeeded in doing was making the cabin a shambles.

Another day of bad weather and a lot of rain passed.

Too close for comfort.

I started wondering how many times during those three years I'd said, 'Another day and soon it will be over . . . only a few days to go.' Each morning I'd say, 'Let's get through another day' and hope it'd be a good one. But now I didn't care whether it was good or bad, I only had a few days to go. For something to do I decided to count up in the log the number of days I'd actually spent at sea and the total came to 500; I'd spent nearly 50 per cent of the time away at sea! All day I kept saying, 'Five hundred days . . . I've spent five hundred days of my life on this boat!' Then one more day was gone.

On the fifth day we had only 90 miles to go. I could pick up Brisbane radio broadcasts again and this really made me realise that I was nearly home. The weather forecaster said, 'Seas rough with waves to three metres. Wind southeast. Strong wind warning still current.' Thanks, but I knew that just from looking outside! The broadcaster continued on with reports of massive flooding at the Gold Coast from the rain and that more torrential rain was expected. But I had thoughts only of just one or two more days at sea and it will all be over.

I settled on a plan to anchor in Moreton Bay and go home until the 16th when I would take *Acrohc* up the river. While I was waiting I could see a doctor about my rash which had more or less cleared up except for five stubborn spots on my bottom (I was out of antibiotics by then).

The sixth day started with good winds decreasing to a nicely normal 20 knots or so. By evening I had switched to the last chart I would use, the one of Moreton Bay—the very same one I used to leave the bay. I was right on the edge of the chart, still 30 miles out to sea, but nonetheless on it. I'd been waiting for that moment for a long time. Now all I had to do was hold against that southerly current for the night so that I could enter the bay the next morning. I heard the weather man say, 'Good weather expected,' and settled down for my last night at sea.

On the two o'clock night check the Cape Moreton light came into view—the same light which saw me out three years earlier was now leading me in. Next morning I still couldn't see land and the wind was gradually dying. The current, however, was getting stronger so we sailed almost due north to compensate for the drift. I just couldn't let it carry us south. I had to arrive no further south than Brisbane no matter what to tie the belt of my circumnavigation. It had to be Brisbane! We were still 20 miles from land when I started motoring but soon I saw the top of Moreton Island and then behind it, the mainland; Brisbane, home at last!

Before noon I passed Cape Moreton. I tried to contact the shore by VHF to let my family know I was back but something was wrong with it and I couldn't get through (although I always stored it in a plastic box the condensation had finally got to it).

I thought no-one knew of my arrival but I later learned that I had been spotted by the lighthouse keeper and he had already contacted my family and a television station. To enter the bay I took a last short cut that took me close to the shore, where the chart showed a shallow

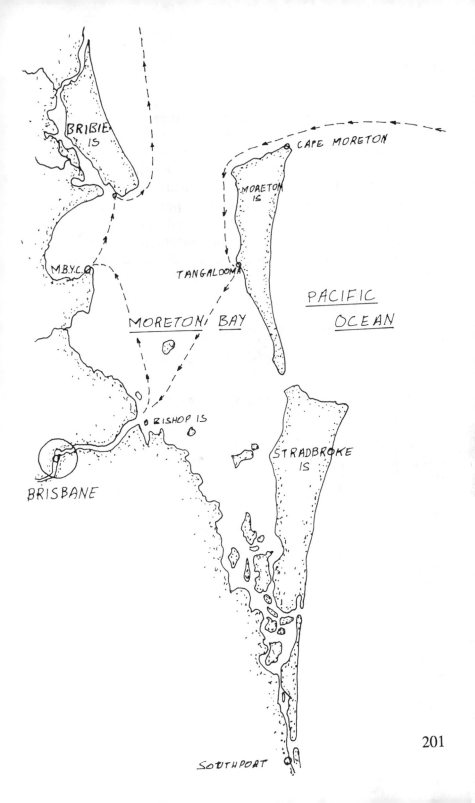

BRIBIE IS

CAPE MORETON

MORETON IS

M.B.Y.C.

TANGALOOMA

PACIFIC OCEAN

MORETON BAY

BISHOP IS

STRADBROKE IS

BRISBANE

SOUTHPORT

201

passage. The water was turbulent from the current but it was no use looking at the depth-sounder. I could see the bottom clearly enough. Too clearly perhaps. Maybe I should have used the deeper passage. But my luck held that time and we got through without touching the bottom. I wondered if my grounding jinx had finally lifted.

I was almost out of fuel but I only had a little way to go to a good anchorage at a place on Moreton Island called Tangalooma. As I was a few days early I could leave *Acrohc* anchored and catch a ferry home to see my family . . . and a doctor (despite my excitement I didn't forget my rash).

FLUTTERING SHEARWATER

After I'd anchored, I used the radio on another yacht to call the authorities and my family. They were really excited and wanted to come over to see me straight away but I explained that they would have to wait until I'd been cleared. I had also been told by the authorities that I wasn't to go ashore until I'd seen the Immigration officers—I had mentioned that I wanted a doctor and this had rather alarmed them.

I was terribly tired so I tried to get some sleep. I was also feeling a bit sick and funny but I put it down to being excited. I was trying to sleep despite the funny sick feeling when I heard a loud engine noise.

It was a big launch with strong spotlights and lots of people with all sorts of cameras. They were expecting to see a radiant sailor and wanted to ask lots of questions. Silvio was also on board but I wasn't to come into contact with anyone before Immigration had cleared me.

They left me alone after an hour even more excited than I'd been before. (Silvio was to come back the next morning.)

I tried to sleep again but soon after I'd settled down another noisy launch came up. This time it was Immigration. They'd hurried over to the island because they'd been told I had a 'disease' but I explained to them what I had wasn't serious enough to quarantine me. We completed the paperwork and soon I was left on my own again. I still felt funny but I was so tired that I soon fell asleep.

Early next morning a helicopter arrived from one of the television stations and then another. After breakfast two more helicopters arrived. There was just no way of avoiding the media as the Council had hoped. Anyway it made no difference to me when they got their story.

Then one man I really wanted to see turned up, the doctor from the island's resort. He took me back to his practice and gave me some of the much needed antibiotics.

When Silvio arrived back at the island, I told him that I'd decided not to go home before the Saturday; I'd been away for nearly three years so I could surely wait two more days so that I could 'arrive home' on *Acrohc* and not on some ferry.

The resort provided us with a nice apartment and the run of the place at no charge. They also provided a 'fake' reception for the media to meet me. It was held on the beach and was complete with girls with armfuls of flowers, platters of seafood and bottles of champagne.

On the Friday *Acrohc* and I left Moreton Island and motored across the Bay. Within a few hours we arrived at our start/finish line, tying the belt of the circumnavigation. There was no celebration here. Here where it had really all started, we were alone, just as we had been for all that time at sea. I took the smoke flare out, pulled the cord and . . . nothing happened. I stared at it—it just had to go off—I'd been thinking about this moment for years!

I was holding the can and starting to curse it when all of a sudden it lit. The thick yellow smoke billowed out and was carried away by the wind just as I had been, three years before. Now I was happy.

I also had the urge to stop there and leave *Acrohc* where I felt she belonged. I thought of drilling a hole in her bottom and leaving her to rest peacefully out there in her element. But I didn't and we continued on, motoring our way peacefully up the river to the small island where Silvio was to meet us where we'd spend the night.

So, it was a rainy Saturday morning when *Acrohc* began her last sail. We were due at the reception at 2.00pm. I even faked engine failure for a while as I was determined to arrive exactly on time.

There were a lot of people waiting to greet us and a brass band was playing (although in the noise and confusion I didn't even hear it). Navy cadets were standing in line to salute our arrival and all my family was there.

A warm welcome by the people of Brisbane, the family and the Lord Mayor.

I was formally greeted by the Lord Mayor and was asked to make a speech. There was also a press conference.

After the formalities I ignored the antibiotics and toasted to *Acrohc* with my family.

When I left, some two hours later, *Acrohc* looked sad. She had a lot of onlookers but no-one really understood what she had meant to me.

GENERAL PARTICULARS OF SHIP

OFFICIAL NO.: 851399	NAME: ACROHC AUSTRALIS		HOME PORT: BRISBANE
CALL SIGN: –	YEAR OF REGISTRATION: 1984	PLACE OF CONSTRUCTION: Brisbane	
YEAR OF COMPLETION: 1984	TYPE: Pleasure Yacht		BUILD: Multi-Chine
STEM: Curved	STERN: Transom		RIGGING: Sloop
NUMBER OF — DECKS: 1 BULKHEADS: 2 MASTS: 1		PRINCIPAL MATERIAL OF CONSTRUCTION: Aluminium	
LENGTH: 3.55 m	MAXIMUM BREADTH: 1.5 m		MOULDED DEPTH AMIDSHIPS: 0.8 m
BRAKE POWER: – kW	INDICATED POWER: – kW	SHAFT POWER: – kW	ESTIMATED SPEED: – kn

PARTICULARS OF PROPULSION

METHOD: Sail Only	POWER TRANSMISSION: –
NUMBER AND TYPE OF ENGINE(S): –	NUMBER AND TYPE OF BOILER(S): –

PARTICULARS OF TONNAGE

THE TONNAGES OF THE SHIP IN ACCORDANCE WITH ITS..
TONNAGE CERTIFICATE ARE —   *(Type)*

GROSS TONNAGE:.. NET/REGISTER TONNAGE:............................

ALTERNATIVE TONNAGES (IF ANY):..

CERTIFICATION

I,.....R.C.T..Bergsma.................... REGISTRAR (OR DEPUTY REGISTRAR) OF SHIPS, CERTIFY THAT THE SHIP, PARTICULARS OF WHICH ARE SET OUT ABOVE, IS DULY REGISTERED UNDER THE SHIPPING REGISTRATION ACT 1981 AND THAT THOSE PARTICULARS, AND THE PARTICULARS OF OWNERSHIP AND PARTICULARS OF REGISTERED AGENT THAT ARE SET OUT BELOW ALONGSIDE TODAY'S DATE AND AUTHENTICATED BY MY SIGNATURE, ARE IN ACCORDANCE WITH THE RELE-VANT ENTRY IN THE AUSTRALIAN REGISTER OF SHIPS.

DATED: 18 October 1984

....
Registrar (or Deputy Registrar) of Ships

P8/1749

D.H.Clarke
"Gables"
Woolverstone
Ipswich
Suffolk IP9 1BA
England

ANALYSIS OF "ACROHC AUSTRALIS" RECORD-BREAKING VOYAGE

by
D.H. CLARKE
(Nautical consultant to the Guinness Book of Records)

The first vessel to be sailed single-handed around the world was Joshua Slocum's *Spray*, 1895-1898. She measured 11.2m (36'9") length overall (L.O.A.). Since then more than 140 men and women have sailed alone around the world in craft ranging in size from the largest, a trimaran 21.28m (69'10") L.O.A., to the smallest, an open boat, 5.72m (18'9") gunter yawl *Chidiock Tichborne*, American Webb Chiles, 1978-1984. Even smaller, although approximately half the voyage was made with a girl companion, was the British 5.59m (18'4") sloop *Super Shrimp*, in which Shane Acton circumnavigated, 1972-1980.

Such was the wide range of sizes of vessels attempting transoceanic records than in the 'seventies it became necessary to divide them into groups, each with an easily remembered name.

SMALL   [Tiny size: Under 4 metres (13' 1½") L.O.A.
           [Midget size: from 4.01 to 6.50 (21'4") L.O.A.
           [Medium size: from 6.51 to 15.50 (50'10") L.O.A.

LARGE   [Major size: from 15.51 to 24.50 (80'5") L.O.A.
           [Giant size: over 24.50 metres L.O.A.

The derivation of T.I.N.Y. — This Is Not Yachting — was an attempt on my part at cynical humour, because quite frankly I was not too keen on encouraging the sport to this dangerous extreme. It made no difference. When there is a possibility of breaking a record in the Blue Water Game (B.W.G.), and lack of funds prevents the use of a larger vessel, then even a tiny size begins to seem attractive. And so, I'm afraid, this class is now very competitive.

The earliest transocean attempt in a tiny craft was made by American William Andrews in 1888. In the 3.9m (12'9") lateen-rigged *Dark Secret* he set sail from Boston towards England, but gave up after 62 days. He tried again in the 3.96m (13'0) gaff cutter *Phantom Ship* in 1898 (abandoned after 34 days), and in 1899 with the 3.66m (12'0) gaff sloop *Doree* (only 21 days this time). The first successful E-W Atlantic crossing in a tiny sized craft was made by John Riding (G.B.) in his 3.66m (12'0) Bermudan sloop *Sjø Äg*, 1964-1965: Plymouth-Azores-Bermuda-Newport (Azores to Bermuda taking 67 days). The first W-E crossing was made by Irishman Bill Verity in 1966: 3.66m (12'0) Bermudan sloop *Nonoalca*, from Fort Lauderdale to Tralee, Eire, in 66 days.

Since those dates, many attempts in ever-decreasing L.O.A. measurements have been made, some successful, most aborted for one reason or another. The current "smallest" records for the Atlantic are:

E-W: 1.79m (5'10 1/2") fibreglass "barrel" *Toniky-Noo*;
Eric Peters (G.B.), Las Palmas to Guadeloupe in 46 days, 1982-1983.
W-E: 2.717m (8'11") *God's Tear*; Wayne Dickinson (U.S.A.) Point Allerton, Mass., to Aranmore, N.W. Eire in 142 days, 1982-1983.

The Pacific has not tempted so many but, surprisingly, there has been more loss of life than in the Atlantic. The first attempt, and the first success in a tiny size, was again made by John Riding. In 1973 having crossed the Pacific from San Diego to New Zealand, he set out for Australia across the Tasman Sea; he was never heard of again. So *Sjø Äg* was the first tiny size to sail half-way around the world, 1964-1973.

The current record "smallest" for the Pacific (no eastwards voyage has yet been attempted) is held by Gerry Spiess (U.S.A.) and his 3.05m (10'0) sloop *Yankee Girl*: Long Beach, California, to Sydney in 105 sailing days, averaging 70 m.p.d., with a fastest noon-to-noon run of 130 miles. These are the fastest speeds achieved by a transoceanic tiny-sized craft to date.

After John Riding, American Bill Dunlop also attempted a circumnavigation — in his much smaller 2.762m (9'0 3/4") sloop *Wind's Will*, in which he had already crossed the Atlantic, from Portland, Maine, to Falmouth in 76 days, 1982. He set out from Portland in July 1983, and was through the Panama Canal by December. He crossed most of the Pacific without any difficulties, and departed from the Cook Islands for Brisbane. His last message, in a margarine container washed ashore on a Queensland beach, indicated he was marooned on an island without food; it was dated October 16, 1984. Nothing has been heard of him since. However, if, as seems likely, he was shipwrecked on a Great Barrier Reef atoll, then *Wind's Will* had already crossed the Pacific and is the smallest to do so. It is possible that this "smallest" record may yet be proved.

Since 1965 so many attempts had been made to beat "smallest" records that in 1983 I decided a ruling on length measurement should be made in order to prevent the dangers on increasing internal and deck capacities by the use of overhangs. (I even had one request for a ruling about carrying supplies on a towed raft!). So since 1983 the following has been circulated whenever possible to potential "smallest" participants.

Length overall measurement of tiny sized craft, in which a transoceanic "smallest" record is to be attempted, is calculated as follows: the distance between two perpendiculars which touch the fore and aft extremities of the vessel that are part of the main hull. The only extensions allowable are a reefing (or hinged) bowsprit, and a removable, transom-hung rudder. Items such as pulpits, pushpits, outboard (unless stowed inboard), outboard brackets, pintles (or gudgeons), bow or stern fenders (either anti-chafe or buoyancy), backstay or bobstay attachments, anchor fairlead overhang, or any other extension to the hull will be included in the L.O.A. measurement. In the event of the beam of the craft exceeding the L.O.A., the higher figures will exclude the vessel from the "smallest" category, but may come within the requirements. of a multihull. The L.O.A. of any towed container, raft or float will be added to the length of the parent vessel. A statement of the L.O.A. according to the above ruling, measured by a responsible person (preferably a boatbuilder, shipwright, etc.), and sworn before a notary, deposited with Guinness Superlatives Ltd. (or myself) before departure, will ensure recognition if the voyage is successful. Reductions of less than 3 centimetres (1 ⅛ inches) from the previous record L.O.A. "smallest" will not be considered.

Unfortunately Serge was unaware of this ruling when he began his circumnavigation. Over the years—and I have been adjudicating these matters for Guinness Superlative Ltd. since 1970—one learns to be flexible about records in the B.W.G.. One day, no doubt, there will be a central organisation who will pontificate at great length, but for now I have to do the best I can—mainly because I am the only person in the world who has bothered to study these transoceanic problems.

Acrohc Australis measures 3.607m (11'10") between perpendiculars. The 63 cm divided bowsprit could be easily hinged, so this has not been counted. The rudder could be easily removable, so this, too, has not been counted. The outboard, unhappily, must be added to the L.O.A., so the official length of the craft for record-breaking purposes, is 3.607m L.O.A. plus 0.563m overhangs = total L.O.A. 4.17 (13'7 ¾). However, most people will think only of the obvious length—just over 3 ½ metres —and to hell with theory! Which is fair enough for now, until the next "smallest" sets forth. By then I hope the ruling I have set out above will be widely known, for despite the financial attractions of sailing a "smallest" into the record book, I hope some sense of proportion will be retained in this very dangerous aspect of the B.W.G.

Whatever I may say about measurement does not detract one jot from Serge Testa's magnificient achievement.

D.H. CLARKE

© Copyright 1987 D.H.Clarke

Note: Entered in the Guinness Book of Records as 3.6m - 11' 10".

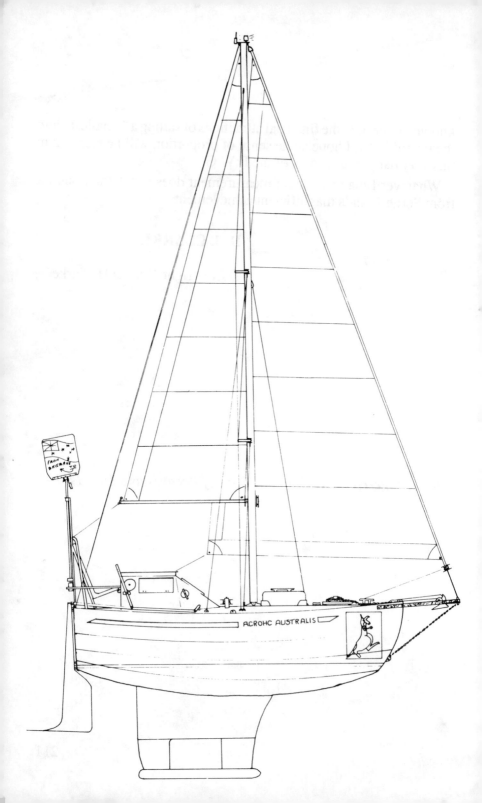

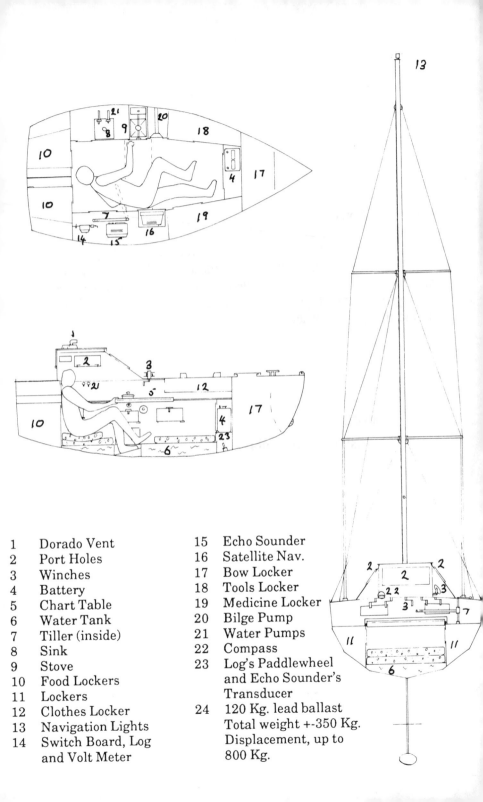

1	Dorado Vent	15	Echo Sounder
2	Port Holes	16	Satellite Nav.
3	Winches	17	Bow Locker
4	Battery	18	Tools Locker
5	Chart Table	19	Medicine Locker
6	Water Tank	20	Bilge Pump
7	Tiller (inside)	21	Water Pumps
8	Sink	22	Compass
9	Stove	23	Log's Paddlewheel
10	Food Lockers		and Echo Sounder's
11	Lockers		Transducer
12	Clothes Locker	24	120 Kg. lead ballast
13	Navigation Lights		Total weight +-350 Kg.
14	Switch Board, Log		Displacement, up to
	and Volt Meter		800 Kg.

TELEX

Congratulations, Sergio, on your epic solo voyage round the world in your self-designed boat. I understand you have set a world record for the smallest boat used in such a venture. Certainly you had to display remarkable courage, skill and endurance. It is fitting that your achievement be publicly acknowledged at this civic reception being given by the Lord Mayor in your honour. We are all proud of you and glad that you returned home safely.

R.J.L. HAWKE
(Prime Minister of Australia)

Acrohc Australis
June 1984 – May 1987